Sermons from the Life of
SAINT JOHN CHRYSOSTOM

T0334811

ST VLADIMIR'S SEMINARY PRESS
Popular Patristics Series
Number 2

The Popular Patristics Series published by St Vladimir's Seminary Press provides readable and accurate translations of a wide range of early Christian literature to a wide audience—students of Christian history to lay Christians reading for spiritual benefit. Recognized scholars in their fields provide short but comprehensive and clear introductions to the material. The texts include classics of Christian literature, thematic volumes, collections of homilies, letters on spiritual counsel, and poetical works from a variety of geographical contexts and historical backgrounds. The mission of the series is to mine the riches of the early Church and to make these treasures available to all.

Series Editor
BOGDAN BUCUR

Associate Editor
IGNATIUS GREEN

* * *

Series Editor
1999–2020
JOHN BEHR

Sermons from the Life of
SAINT JOHN CHRYSOSTOM

Translation and Introduction by
DAVID C. FORD

ST VLADIMIR'S SEMINARY PRESS
YONKERS, NEW YORK
2023

Publisher's Cataloging-in-Publication
(Provided by Cassidy Cataloguing Services, Inc.).

Names: John Chrysostom, Saint, -407, author. | Ford, David C., 1949-, translator, writer of added commentary.

Title: Sermons from the life of Saint John Chrysostom / Saint John Chrysostom ; translation, introduction, and notes by David C. Ford.

Other titles: Homilies. Selections. English

Description: Yonkers, NY : St Vladimir's Seminary Press, [2023] | Series: St. Vladimir's Seminary

Press Popular patristics series. | Includes bibliographical references.

Identifiers: ISBN: 978-0-88141-729-6 (paperback) | 978-0-88141-730-2 (eBook) | LCCN: 2023942890

Subjects: LCSH: John Chrysostom, Saint, -407--Sermons. | Orthodox Eastern Church--Sermons. | Christian saints--Sermons. | Sermons, Greek--Translations into English. | Church history--Primitive and early church, ca. 30-600. | BISAC: RELIGION / Christian Church / History. | RELIGION / Christianity / Saints & Sainthood. | RELIGION / Sermons / Christian.

Classification: LCC: BR65.C43 E5 2023 | DDC: 252/.019--dc23

COPYRIGHT © 2023 BY
ST VLADIMIR'S SEMINARY PRESS
575 Scarsdale Road, Yonkers, NY 10707
1-800-204-2665 | www.svspresss.com

ISBN: 978-0-88141-729-6 (paperback) | 978-0-88141-730-2 (eBook)

The views in the introduction and the notes of this book do not
necessarily reflect those of St Vladimir's Seminary.

The publication of this book was made possible in part by generous donations from Dr Donald J. Tamulonis, Jr; Peter Coucheron-Aamot; Nicole Green; Rev. Emmanuel Mantzouris; and Ellen Miller.

Contents

Abbreviations

NPNF[1]   The Nicene and Post-Nicene Fathers, Series 1. Edited by Philip Schaff. New York, 1886–1889. 14 vols. Repr., Peabody, MA: Hendrickson, 1994.

PG   Patrologia Graeca. Edited by J.-P. Migne. 162 vols. Paris, 1857–1886.

SC   Sources chrétiennes. Paris: Cerf. 1942–

Introduction

This is the sixth volume in the Popular Patristics Series devoted to works by St John Chrysostom (*c.* 349–407) and, I am told, a seventh is on the way—making him, along with St Basil the Great, the most popular author in the entire series. This is only fitting, since we have more from him than from virtually any other of the Church Fathers. In addition, most of his works were homilies preached to the common people in the great cosmopolitan centers of Antioch and Constantinople—sermons that were recorded by stenographers as he preached them. And even after any editing he may have done with the manuscripts, the conversational flavor of his preaching is retained. This makes his works all the more accessible and endearing to the modern reader, as he speaks from his heart to the hearts of his flock in very direct, penetrating ways.

This volume contains nine of Chrysostom's homilies that were all preached at dramatic moments in his life, beginning with the words he spoke on the day of his ordination to the holy priesthood, in Antioch in February of 386, and ending with the words he spoke in Constantinople, in October of 403, after his unexpected return from his first, very brief period in exile. So these homilies span most of his time in active ministry. Through them, much of his story in these years is told. And because he shares in them his personal responses to the swirl of events surrounding him, they provide us with a profound glimpse into the depths of his heart and soul—especially regarding his great love and pastoral care for his beloved flock.

These homilies readily demonstrate his deep love for preaching and his tremendous skill in that art. In his youth, he was trained in the techniques of classical oratory by one of the greatest pagan rhetoricians of the ancient world, Libanius of Antioch. John was flourishing under Libanius' tutelage so wonderfully that Libanius was already grooming him to be his successor. But much to Libanius' chagrin, John, at about the age of twenty, reaffirmed the Christian faith of his youth—which he had imbibed through the example and guidance of his saintly mother, Anthusa—and gave himself wholeheartedly to live for Christ and grow in the Christian life.

Besides being extremely adept at all facets of the art of rhetoric, when John gave himself, his talents, and his training into the hands of Christ in the service of his holy

Church, his eloquence gained the additional power of the Holy Spirit.

Yes, he loved to preach—not only for the sheer joy of the rhetoric, but more importantly, because he loved his people so much. Their attentiveness, their love and appreciation for him—sometimes they would spontaneously break out into applause as he preached—inspired him greatly. As he said once to them:

> When I speak, weariness disappears; when I begin to teach, fatigue also dissipates. Thus neither sickness itself, nor indeed any other obstacle, is able to separate me from your love.... For just as you are hungry to listen to me, so too am I hungry to preach to you.[1]

Indeed, he poured out his life into the hearts and minds and souls of his flock, as we can tell from this declaration in one of his homilies: "For I have vehemently set my heart upon your salvation!"[2] He even spoke of being *enslaved* to his flock, because of their ardent love for him:

> I, too, am a slave—a slave to your love for me. You purchased me, not by casting down silver, but by showing forth your love. I rejoice in this slavery! May I never be loosed from it! For this slavery

---

[1]Quoted by Carl A. Volz, "The Genius of Chrysostom's Preaching," *Christian History* 44 (1994): 24 (original source not given). This entire issue of *Christian History* is devoted to Chrysostom and his life and times.

[2]Homily 43.3 on First Corinthians (NPNF² 12:260).

is better than a crown; this slavery procures the Kingdom of Heaven; this slavery is better than freedom; this slavery prepares for me a throne at the Last Judgment. And this slavery is not a matter of compulsion, but of free choice.

Who would not gladly serve you as a slave, since you are such mad lovers? If I had a heart of stone, you have made it softer than wax.[3]

Since many details of his life are presented in the introductions of the previous five volumes in this series devoted to his writings, I will not rehearse those facts again in this introduction. So instead of a customary twenty- or twenty-five-page introduction, I will present substantial introductions to each of the nine homilies as they are given in chronological order in this book.

Some of the nine homilies in this book have never before been translated and published in English. Others appear in the very distinguished *Nicene and Post-Nicene Fathers* series, edited by Philip Schaff; but those translations were done nearly one hundred and forty years ago, in a lofty kind of Victorian English that is rather archaic and not easily understood by typical readers today. Others have been translated into more modern English, but they are not readily available. In every case, I have consulted the original Greek to bring forth new translations in which I attempt to be as faithful to Chrysostom's meaning

[3] From his *Homily Upon his Return from Asia*, as translated in this volume, 164–165.

and expression in the Greek as possible, while seeking to make sure that each text sounds as clear and eloquent as if English were his first language.

The vast works of our beloved St John Chrysostom continue to be highly valued in the Christian world, especially among Orthodox Christians, who celebrate nearly every Sunday of the year—and in some monasteries, nearly every day of the year—the Divine Liturgy that bears his name. His image is depicted iconographically in nearly every Orthodox Church; his famous Paschal Sermon is read at the midnight Pascha (Easter) service every year; and his memory is celebrated and venerated every year: on November 13 (to commemorate the date of his passing from this life in AD 407, which is transferred from September 14, since this is the feast of the Exaltation of the Cross); on January 27 (to commemorate the date of the translation of his relics back to Constantinople in triumph thirty-one years after he died in exile in eastern Asia Minor); and on January 30 (the date of the triple commemoration of the most illustrious Three Holy Hierarchs—St Basil the Great, St Gregory the Theologian, and St John Chrysostom). And his works remain ever at hand for the catechetical instruction of newcomers to the Faith, and for the ongoing instruction, edification, inspiration, and illumination of the faithful as they seek to live in closer communion with Christ and all his saints.

As just one example of contemporary appreciation for this great Saint, here is what an elder in Russia at the end of the Soviet era, Hierodeacon Benedict (Khodchenkov), said about St John's works: "He who wants to cleanse his mind from the poison of misunderstandings should read all ten volumes of St John Chrysostom."[4]

In light of all of this, it is no wonder that the Orthodox Church praises him in such hymns as these:

Troparion (Tone 8)

> Grace shining forth from your lips like a beacon-fire has enlightened the universe. It has shown to the world the riches of poverty; it has revealed to us the heights of humility. Teaching us by your words, O Father John Chrysostom, intercede before the Word, Christ our God, to save our souls!

Kontakion (Tone 6)

> From Heaven you have received grace divine; and with your lips you teach all men to worship the one God in Trinity. O holy Father John the Golden Mouth, worthily we praise you, for you are indeed our teacher, revealing things divine!

May we in the twenty-first century ever come to know him better—through prayer, especially before his icon, and through reading and meditating upon his golden words. May we come to love him in the same way his flock did in the late fourth century, in response to his tremendous,

---

[4]Quoted by Fr Artemy Vladimirov, "University Years," *Road to Emmaus* 81–82 (Spring/Summer 2020): 39–102, at 89.

undying love for us. And may we be greatly inspired by the power of his eloquence, and by the soul-stirring challenge as well as soothing comfort of his timeless message that is still piercingly relevant in every time and place.

Homily on His Ordination to the Priesthood

A note on the text

This is the first recorded homily by St John Chrysostom that comes down to us. For the previous five years he had served as a deacon in the church in his hometown, the illustrious metropolis of Antioch, the first major Christian center after the Faith began to be spread from Jerusalem. St Luke tells us that *the disciples were first called Christians in Antioch* (Acts 11.26). This is the city where St Paul lived and taught for about a year and a half before being sent forth by prophecy, along with the Apostle Silas, on his first great missionary journey, across Asia Minor. Antioch was still a major Christian center in St John's day, with about half of the population by then being at least nominally Christian.

St John had been ordained a deacon by the archbishop of the church in Antioch, St Meletius (d. 381), in 381, shortly before Meletius went to Constantinople to preside at the Second Ecumenical Council. Meletius died during that council and was succeeded by Flavian (*c.* 320–404) as the new archbishop of Antioch. It was Archbishop Flavian who ordained St John to the priesthood, and so he was in attendance during the preaching of this sermon.

It may seem surprising that St John would say in this sermon that it is the first time he has ever preached publicly. In his late teenage years, he had been trained in classical rhetoric by the brilliant Libanius (314–393), one of the greatest pagan orators in the history of the entire ancient Greek and Roman world. Libanius was expecting John to be his successor as teacher of rhetoric in Antioch, but he later lamented that the Christians "stole him away" from him. Indeed, John apparently quite suddenly turned from the "sophistry" of pagan oratory—and perhaps from studies for a career in the profession of law—to devote his life to Christ and his Church, when he was about twenty years old, around the year 369. He had been baptized as a child and had been raised by his saintly mother, Anthusa, so he was coming back to the Faith of his upbringing.

It is interesting that about seventeen years passed before St John could begin to use his tremendous native talent for oratory, along with his magnificent training in rhetoric, in public service in the Church. It may have been difficult for him to be patient about that, especially after being made a deacon and having an active role in the life of the Church in Antioch—but not including preaching, since it was not the custom at that time and place for deacons to preach.

But in this sermon he hints that he had been content to remain on the sidelines, saying, "I will prepare to enter 'the stadium' to teach, even though I have never before undertaken such contests, having always remained in the ranks of the listeners, keeping to myself, and being silent."

And we know that when John was first considered for ordination to the priesthood, when he was in his early twenties, he firmly resisted, protesting that he was not worthy or capable of that exceedingly high office. He later wrote about that incident in his famous dialogue/ essay, *On the Priesthood*,[1] in which he made very clear his self-understanding that he was far too unworthy, incapable, and unprepared to assume such an awesome responsibility, for he rightly considered the holy priesthood in Christ's Church to be the most important position on the face of the earth.

After serving as a deacon for about five years, most of that time as a close attendant and assistant to Archbishop Flavian, Deacon John was considered once again for priestly ordination. This time, being older, and having such valuable experience serving under his beloved archbishop, he relented and obeyed Flavian's wishes. But as he says very movingly in this sermon preached on his ordination day, as he publicly addresses the flock in the Great Church in the great city of Antioch for the first time, "For you and for your love, I will face this situation into

---

[1]St John Chrysostom, *Six Books on the Priesthood*, trans. Graham Neville, Popular Patristics Series 1 (Crestwood, NY: St Vladimir's Seminary Press, 1977 and reprints).

which I could not have been more violently or tyrannically compelled. I will venture to speak, despite my lack
of experience."

After John's ordination to the priesthood, Archbishop
Flavian very quickly made him the principal preacher in
the Great Church of Antioch. John would hold this position for the next twelve years, warmly and strongly sup-
ported by his flock, who loved him because he so loved
them, always pouring out his heart in his preaching for
their spiritual growth in Christ—and ultimately, for their
salvation.

We already can see his very high esteem for the Christians of Antioch in this, his ordination sermon. He especially shows here his high estimation and appreciation
of the importance and efficacy of their prayers for him,
describing their "prayers illuminating my way in the
midst of my perplexity, just as lightning illumines the
darkness." Furthermore, near the end of the sermon, he
says to the flock,

> But if you think of me, as one would remember
> a certain miserable wretch [*amblōthridiou*], pray
> that great power will come upon me from on
> high. For if formerly we needed protection . . .
> much more now do we need your helping hand,
> your myriad of prayers.

We also see in this sermon St John's tremendously high
appreciation for his archbishop, as he praises his virtues
extensively. Indeed, Archbishop Flavian is recognized in

the Orthodox Church as St Flavian of Antioch. His feast day is September 27.

On the following pages, readers will encounter what St John the Golden-Mouth said on that momentous day when he began his preaching career.

Homily on His Ordination to the Priesthood[2]

So then! The things that have happened to us—are they true? Have these things really occurred? Or is it all an illusion?

Are these present things a dream of the night? Yet it is not nighttime! Truly it is daytime; and are we not all awake and alert?

Yet who can believe these things?—that being daytime, when men are alert and watchful, a mere common lad,[3] having no merit,[4] has been raised to such a high position of authority?

<hr>

[2]The original Greek text is found in PG 48:693–700; a critical Greek text is found in SC 272:367–419.

[3]Greek: *meirakiskos eutelēs.*

[4]We have a glimpse here of St John's deep humility, calling himself "a mere common lad having no merit," even though he has brilliant talent and training and is thirty-seven years old!

That something like this might happen at night, in a dream, is no wonder. Sometimes it happens that certain people who are crippled in body, and not even having necessary food, will lie down to sleep and dream that they have become nimble and good-looking, enjoying being seated at a royal table. But alas! It was only a dream, vain and vanishing! Such is the nature of dreams: they work fantasies and enjoy playing tricks on us.

By contrast, such things do not happen in the day-time, in the realm of reality. It is manifest that everything indeed has happened; the deed has indeed been done!— even though the things you have beheld are more beyond belief than dreams.

And now this great city, so populous—this great and marvelous multitude—has gathered near me in my little-ness, as if expecting to hear something great and noble from us. Yet even if my powers of eloquence were like endlessly rushing rivers and gushing fountains, the fearful sight of the crowds who have gathered here would imme-diately stop my words in their course and drive them back to their source. But when our powers of speech are not like rivers or fountains—indeed, they are not even com-parable to the slightest drizzle—how could they not be dried up by fear, at least to some degree?

Is this not like what happens with the human body? And what is that? It often happens, as we hold things in our hands and grasp them with our fingers, that out of some fear our nerves become paralyzed, the strength of our flesh dissolves, and we let go of everything. This is what I fear will happen at this moment—that all my thoughts, small and common though they are, which I have gathered with much labor to share with you, will vanish from my memory because of my agony, leaving my mind as empty as a desert.

Therefore I beseech you all alike, both those who are rulers and those who are ruled: through your prayers, change into inspired boldness the agony you have thrown me into by your eagerly gathering to hear me. Implore the one who gives words to His evangelists with much power to give us the discourse to bring forth, as He opens our mouth.[5] It will not be laborious for you, as numerous as you are, to strengthen once again the soul of a lad[6] held fast by fear.

In fulfilling this request of ours, you will be doing what is just. And for you and for your love, I will face this situation into which I could not have been more violently or tyrannically compelled. I will venture to speak, despite my lack of experience. I will prepare to enter "the stadium" to teach, even though I have never before undertaken such contests, having always remained in the ranks of the listeners, keeping to myself, and being silent.

What sort of man could be so hard-hearted, so unfeeling, as to remain silent before such a gathering as this—finding here such warmth, such eagerness to listen—even

---

[5] St John often uses the royal "we" in his preaching when referring to himself.

[6] Greek: *meirakiskou.*

if he were more incompetent in public speaking than all other men?

We desire, therefore, as we are about to speak for the first time in the Church, to give the firstfruits of this tongue of ours to God, the one who has given this gift to us. And so it must be! For not only are the firstfruits of the crops and the winepress owed to the Word, but also, and more especially, the firstfruits of speech. And the more this fruit is near and dear to us, the more pleasing it is to Him, our most honored God.

The grapevines and the corn bring forth fruit from the bosom of the earth, nurtured by the waters streaming from the clouds and cultivated by the hands of those working the earth; while the holy hymn is born of a devout soul, nourished by a good conscience, which God receives into the treasuries of Heaven. And as the soul is superior to the earth, so is this fruit better than the former.

Therefore one of the prophets, a man marvelous and great, whose name was Hosea, when speaking to those wishing to appease the anger of God, advised them to make an offering, not of herds of cattle, neither such-and-such measure of wheat, neither a turtledove nor a pigeon, nor any other such thing, but what? *Bring to Him words*, he says (Hos 14.2).

And what kind of sacrifice is a word?—someone may fairly ask. The greatest there can be, my beloved ones, and the most august, better than all others! And who says these things? One versed in an exact knowledge of all these things, the noble and great David. For when he was offering to God a sacrifice of thanksgiving for a victory he had won in warfare, he did so by saying, *I will praise the name of my God with a song; I will magnify Him with praise* (Ps 68.30). And to indicate the excellence of this sacrifice, he added, *And this shall please God more than a bull with horns and hooves* (v. 31).

Therefore, I wanted to present today such sacrifices, to redden the spiritual altar with streams of mystical blood. But alas! What is to become of me? A wise man closes my mouth, frightening me by saying, *Beautiful praise does not come from the mouth of a sinner* (Eccl 15.9). Just as with garlands, not only the flowers need to be pure but also the hands of the one weaving them, so also with the sacred hymns—not only do the words need to be godly, but also the soul of the one offering them. Yet our soul is polluted, filled with many sins; so I have no confidence in speaking.

Under these circumstances, it is not only this law that closes my mouth, but another one even more ancient, laid down before that one. For this same David, who spoke to us earlier about sacrifices, also said, *Praise the Lord from the heavens, praise Him in the highest*; and a little later, *Praise the Lord from the earth* (Ps 148.1 and 7). In summoning both kinds of creatures—those above and those below; those impalpable and those perceptible; those visible and those not visible; those beyond the heavens and those under the heavens—he forms one choir from both. Thus they are all summoned to hymn the King of all. David, however, did not summon the sinner, but rather excluded him from the chorus.

In order to make what I am saying more clear to you, I will bring us back to that psalm: *Praise the Lord from the heavens*, it says; *praise Him in the highest. Praise Him, all His angels; praise Him, all His hosts* (Ps 148.1–2). Do you see the angels giving praise, and the archangels, and the cherubim and seraphim, and the other heavenly powers? For when he says, "all the powers," he is including all the crowd of people above. But do you see a sinner among them? How could you? For how would it be possible to see a sinner in Heaven?

Now let us descend, and let us lead you to the earth, to another part of the choir that has been gathered together, and there also you will not see a sinner: *Praise the Lord from the earth, ye dragons and all deeps… beasts and all cattle, creeping things and winged birds* (Ps 148.7 and 10). It is not falsely, it is not without reason, that I have been silenced by these words. The thoughts of my mind have become confused; I have come to bitter tears and great lamentation.

For what could be more pitiable than this? Tell me! Scorpions, and vipers, and dragons are called to give praise to the one who made them; only the sinner is left out of this sacred choir—and rightly so. For sin is an evil and merciless beast; it does not show forth its wickedness upon the bodies of its fellow-slaves, but it pours out its evil poison against the glory of the Master. *Because of you*, it says, *My name is blasphemed among the nations* (Is 52.5, LXX).

This is why the prophet drives the sinner far away, expelling him from the inhabited world as if from his sacred homeland. Just so, the skilled musician removes from his harp the string that makes unharmonious sounds, so that the harmony of the rest of the instrument is not destroyed. And likewise, the doctor versed in his art cuts off the gangrenous member, lest the afflicted member spread its disease to the remaining members of the body. The prophet did just that in cutting off the sinner from the whole body of creation, as if he were an unharmonious string or a diseased member of the body.

What, therefore, would be appropriate for us to do? Exiled as we are, cut off as we are, it is entirely needful for us to keep silent. Should we, then, keep silent? Tell me! Is no one providing a way for us to hymn our Master? Have we called for your prayers in vain? Have we fled in vain to the protection of your intercessions? No, not in vain! May it not be so!

For I have found, yes, I have found another way to offer praise, with your prayers illuminating my way in the midst of my perplexity, just as lightning illumines the darkness. I will praise my fellow-servants.[7] For it is permissible to praise one's like-minded fellow-servants—for in praising them, the glory redounds entirely to the Master. That He is glorified thereby, Christ Himself shows forth in saying, *Let your light shine among men, so that in seeing your good works, they will glorify your Father in Heaven* (Mt 5.16).

So behold this different kind of praise,[8] which it is possible for a sinner to give without transgressing the law.

[7]Greek: *homodoulous.*
[8]Greek: *doxologias.*

Which one, therefore, which one of our fellow-servants will we extol? Which one? None other than the common teacher of our fatherland—and through our land, the whole world.[9] Just as he has taught you to stand firm in the truth even unto death, so likewise you have taught other men to give up life itself rather than godliness.

Would you desire us, therefore, to plait a garland of praise for him? I have desired to do so also, but I see before me the vast ocean of his good works, and I fear that my feeble voice, once brought down to the depths of them, will not come back up. For it would be necessary to discourse about great deeds of old, of journeys and vigils, of dedicated care and judgments full of wisdom, of noble battles, of trophies upon trophies and victories upon victories, all of which are beyond the power not only of my own, but of any human tongue, to describe and praise worthily. Only an apostolic voice, moved by the Holy Spirit, would have the power to speak and teach adequately.

So, moving past these things, we will come to a safer sea, which a small craft can sail upon for a little while.

Come, therefore, and let us direct our words towards his self-control. Let us speak of how he eats in moderation, how he despises luxury, how he scorns an extravagant table—which he grew up with to a great degree in his childhood home.[10]

---

[9]Referring to their own Archbishop Flavian, who had just ordained him. Of course, the bishop is present, hearing these words.

[10]Archbishop Flavian grew up in a wealthy family, and upon inheriting great wealth as a young man, he devoted it to the service of the Church and the poor.

It is no wonder for one brought up in poverty to adopt a harsh and difficult way of life. Poverty itself, as his constant companion and fellow-traveler, lightens his burden every day.

But for anyone who has been the master of wealth, it is not easy for him to disengage from it, since a swarm of passions has doubtless enveloped such a soul. Such a dense and dark cloud of passions does not allow him to look up towards Heaven. Rather, it forces him downwards, keeping him gaping at the earth.

There is nothing, indeed there is nothing else that blocks our way to Heaven as much as wealth, and the evils that so often come with it. This is not my word; Christ Himself brought forth this pronouncement, saying, *It is easier for a camel to pass through the eye of a needle than for a rich man to enter the Kingdom of Heaven* (Mt 19.24).

But behold! This difficult—or rather, impossible—thing becomes possible! What Peter of old was at a loss about, what he sought to learn from the Teacher, this all of us have come to know even more thoroughly through experience. For not only do the wealthy rise to Heaven, but he [Archbishop Flavian] guides the entire populace there. And this, despite his wealth, and other things that were no less obstacles than that—his youth, and his premature orphanhood, which are especially sufficient to beguile all men, full as these things are of allurements, like enchanted potions prepared with poison.

But our teacher has prevailed over all these things; he has laid hold of Heaven; he has made the philosophy there his own.[11] He did not embrace the splendor of this present life, neither did he look to the illustriousness of his forebears. Or rather, he did look to the illustriousness of his forebears, but not the ones to whom he was bound by ties beyond his control.[12] Instead, he has drawn close to the ones with whom he chose to be united in godliness. This is indeed how it has happened with him.

He has looked to the patriarch Abraham; he has looked to the great Moses, who, despite being raised in a royal household, being accustomed to partaking of a lavish table, being used to the clamorous banquets of the Egyptians—and you know how things were among those barbarians, filled with vanity and ostentation—he scorned all these things and went to the clay, making bricks, desiring to be among the captives and slaves, even though he was a prince, an [adopted] son of the king.

Accordingly, because of this, after he returned to Egypt he was given more authority than he had formerly. For after his time as a fugitive, after his hired service for his father-in-law, after the hardship of living in a foreign land, upon his return he was made protector of the king—or rather, he became a god of the king. For it says, *See, I have made you a god to Pharaoh* (Ex 7.1). He was more splendid than the king, though without having a crown, without being clothed in purple, without driving a golden chariot; and he trampled all his splendor underfoot. For

[11]For Chrysostom, Christianity is the true philosophy.

[12]Referring to his blood relatives, whom he obtained simply through his birth.

as it is written, *All the glory of the king's daughter is within* [herself] (Ps 44.13).

Indeed, after his return he had a scepter, and he commanded not only men, but also the heavens and the earth and the sea, the very nature of air and water, and lakes and springs and rivers. For all the elements became whatever he wished them to become. Creation became transformed in his hands, becoming like a willing servant who is eager, upon seeing the friend of his master, to obey everything the friend commands as if he were the master himself.[13]

This is the one after whom, him whom we are praising modeled himself; he became like him, even from his youth—if he ever was young! I think he never was, since he had such venerable maturity of thought[14] even from when he was in swaddling-clothes. For even when the number of his years was small, he embraced the Christian philosophy whole and entire. As soon as he perceived that our human nature is like a wild vine run to wood, he easily cut short the diseases of the soul with the word of godliness as with a sickle. And as pure, arable land offers to the farmer the opportunity to cast in the seeds, he took the divine seeds and planted them deeply in the earth of his soul. And neither did the heat of the sun wither what sprouted from them, nor did thorns choke the shoots.

This is how he has healed his soul. As for his flesh, he checked its "bounding and leaping" with the medicines

---

[13]Here St John is referring to the ten plagues of Egypt as described in Exodus 7–12, as well as the miraculous crossing of the Red Sea.
[14]Greek: *phronēma*.

of self-control. As if it were a certain impetuous horse, he pulled on the reins, not sparing even "bloodying the mouth" of the passions until he mastered them, guiding them to his goal. Even so, he did not overly strain his body, lest he ruin the powers of the horse and render it unserviceable. Yet neither did he allow it to enjoy too much good health, lest it become soft and rise up against the one reining it in through reason, keeping it sound and in a state of good order.[15]

He was not only like this in his youth, for he also showed himself to be this way in his later years. And now that he is settled in his old age as in a secure harbor, his vigilance is still the same. For youth resembles a raging sea, filled with fierce waves and evil winds, while old age is like a calm harbor, wherein the souls of the elderly have anchored, to enjoy profound security therein.

Yet, as I have said, while he is in enjoyment now, settled in harbor, he remains vigilant no less than those tossed in the midst of the open sea. For he received from Paul the fear that he expressed after having ascended to Heaven, having conversed there, and having touched even the third Heaven: *I fear, lest having preached the gospel to others, I myself may become disapproved* (1 Cor 9.27).

Thus he keeps himself in continual fear, in order to be in continual security. He is always there at the helm, closely watching—not the movements of the stars or the rocks lurking beneath the waves, but rather the attacks of the demons, and the wicked works of the devil, and struggles

[15]Greek: *eutaxia.*

with disruptive thoughts.[16] And surveying his army's encampment, he keeps it all established in security. For not only does he make sure that his ship does not sink; he also does everything he can to make sure that his traveling companions are not threatened by any disturbance. Thanks to his care and wisdom, we voyage entirely with a fair breeze, our sails fully unfurled in the wind.

When we lost our previous spiritual father, who was born for us, we were desolate.[17] Therefore we lamented piteously, even as we hoped for another man like him to receive the episcopal throne.

And as soon as this one appeared and came into our midst,[18] all our despondency vanished like a cloud; all our gloominess disappeared. And not little by little did our sadness dissipate, but all at once, as if that blessed one whom we were mourning had arisen from his coffin and had again ascended the episcopal throne.

---

[16]Greek: *logismōn*. This word, the plural of *logismos*, simply means "thoughts" or "considerations." But in time, *logismos* has come to have in the Christian tradition the technical meaning of unwanted, deleterious thoughts that come not from God but from our disordered passions or from the dark forces of evil. We are all called to be ever "on the lookout" for such thoughts, so we can repulse them quickly through prayer, with the help of God's grace.

[17]This was St Meletius of Antioch, who died as he was presiding at the Second Ecumenical Council, held in Constantinople in 381. [For a homily from his funeral, see St Gregory of Nyssa, *On Death and Eternal Life*, trans. Brian E. Daley, Popular Patristics Series 64 (Yonkers, NY: St Vladimir's Seminary Press, 2022), 110–22.—*Ed.*] He had become archbishop of Antioch in 360.

[18]Referring to Archbishop Flavian, Meletius' immediate successor.

But we have forgotten ourselves, having been carried away beyond proper limits by our love[19] for our father's virtuous deeds—not limits imposed by his virtues, for we have still not begun to extol them properly, but by our youthfulness.

So come now, let us, as if in harbor, bring our words to an end, and be silent once again. Yet I do so, not willingly, but sorrowfully and agonizingly, for I fervently desire to extend my discourse further. But that would be impracticable, my children!

So let us cease pursuing what is beyond reach; let us be content with what we have already said. As it is with precious myrrh, it is not enough to pour it into a basin; one has to dip one's fingers into it to anoint those present, and to fill the air with fragrance. This is what is happening now—not through the power of our words, but through the virtue of *his* righteous deeds.

So let us desist. Let us desist, being overwhelmed by the need for prayer. Let us pray that our common mother, the Church, will remain unshaken and unmoved, and that this father, teacher, shepherd, and pilot will be granted a very long life.

I dare not give a word to you about myself. I dare not count myself among the priests, just as an aborted child cannot be counted among those who are born intact.

But if you think of me, as one would remember a certain miserable wretch,[20] pray that great power will come upon

[19]Greek: *epithymia.*
[20]Greek: *amblōthridiou.*

me from on high. For if formerly we needed protection, while we were living on our own, free from other cares, how much more now, since we have been led into the Church—either through human zeal or through divine grace, I will not be contentious about it—and have put on this severe and heavy yoke, much more now do we need your helping hand, your myriad of prayers, so that we may be able to return intact unto our saving Master what He has entrusted to us, against that day when all those entrusted with talents will be called and led into court to give an account of what they have done with them.

Pray that we not be counted among those bound and cast into darkness, but rather that we be among those worthy of pardon, by the grace and love for mankind[21] of our Lord Jesus Christ, to whom be glory and might and worship, unto ages of ages. Amen.

[21] Greek: *philanthrōpia.*

Second Homily
on the Statues

A note on the text

On the morning of Thursday, February 25, 387, the civil authorities in Antioch announced that Emperor Theodosius had mandated a new, exorbitant tax without any previous warning, which would affect all classes of society. In protest, a highly destructive riot broke out, during which statues of the emperor and his family were torn down and desecrated. Everyone knew that this outrageous act was virtually the same as personally insulting and abusing the emperor, the most powerful figure in the whole world.

An eerie silence fell over the city, as the citizens realized that the emperor might even send troops to raze the city in recompense for this outrage against his authority and his personal honor. Meanwhile the perpetrators of the riot, whom St John calls "certain foreigners, men of mixed ancestry, pernicious, with blood on their hands," were being rounded up, and some of them were already being executed.

This was the tense and dramatic setting for this sermon, which St John preached three days after the riot occurred, on the Sunday immediately before the beginning of Great Lent. Altogether, he would preach twenty-one homilies in this series, known as the *Homilies on the Statues*. This sermon is the second in the series, since St John had already preached the first sermon on the previous Sunday.

In the first part of this sermon, St John pours out his own lament over what had happened, saying that he can scarcely speak because of his grief: "Here I would wish to bring my words to an end, since those whose souls are in anguish have no desire to extend their speaking to a great length." But then, gathering his resolve, his determination to help his people, and knowing that they need some sense of a return to normality to help them deal with the crisis, he exclaims, "This is what I expect to do today: to keep on speaking unto your souls, so that with my words dwelling within you I hope to burst through your cloud of despondency, so that our customary teaching may shine in your minds once again." The "customary teaching" is, in this sermon, his presentation of the lessons to be drawn from and inspired by the appointed epistle reading of the day, which was from 1 Timothy 6. His teaching, a very enlightening discussion of the proper spiritual perspective on wealth and poverty, takes up roughly the last two-thirds of this lengthy homily.

Second Homily
on the Statues[1]

What shall I say? How can I speak? This is a time for tears, not words—a time for lamentation, not discourse; a time for prayer, not oratory. Such is the magnitude of the deeds so daringly done, so incurable the wound, so great the trauma, beyond the healing powers of all our physicians, requiring help from above.

So it was with Job, who, having lost everything, sat on a dunghill. Hearing of this, his friends came, and seeing him from afar, they tore their garments, sprinkled themselves with ashes, and mourned greatly. So also the cities all around us ought to do—to come to our city, and grieve with great sympathy over the events that have happened.

Then, Job sat down on a dunghill; now, our city sits upon a great snare. And just as then the devil leapt upon

[1]PG 49:33–48; NPNF[1] 9:344–54; a modern Greek translation may be found in *Iōannou tou Chrysostomou Erga* [Works of St John Chrysostom], vol. 8 (Athens: Ekdoseis ho Logos, 1973), 43–59.

the flocks and herds and everything that the just man had, so now the devil has descended upon our whole city with Bacchic frenzy.[2]

But then, as well as now, God permitted it—then, to make that just man more brilliant through the magnitude of his trials; and now, to make us more prudent and sober through the extreme severity of this affliction.

Allow me now to mourn over our present state. I have been silent for seven days, just like Job's friends.[3] Allow me to open my mouth today, to bewail this calamity afflicting us all.

Who has worked witchcraft upon us, beloved? Who has envied us malignantly? How has such a change come over us? Nothing was more solemn[4] than our city; but now, nothing is more pitiable. The populace was so well-ordered and gentle; but like a tractable and well-tamed horse that was always obedient in the hands of its master, they have now so suddenly bolted off and have worked such evils as one cannot even dare to mention.

I wail and lament now, not on account of the great magnitude of the expected punishment, but for the extremity of the madness that has overtaken us. For even if the emperor is not struck with a paroxysm of anger, even if he does not punish and torture us, how will we bear, tell me, the shame of what has happened?

---

[2]Bacchus was the Greek god of wine and revelry.

[3]He is referring to the fact that he had not preached since the previous Sunday.

[4]Greek: *semnoteron*.

My word of instruction is cut short now by lamentation. I scarcely have the strength to open my mouth, to part my lips, to move my tongue, to come forth with any words at all. Just like a bridle, the weight of grief checks my tongue and seizes my words before I can say them.

Before now, nothing was more blessed than our city; now, nothing is more barren of happiness. Just as bees buzzing around their hive, so all those dwelling in our city used to amble about the marketplace every day, and everyone called us blessed for being so numerous.

But behold! Now this hive has become a desert. For even as smoke drives bees away, so fear has driven away our bees. And what the prophet said, bewailing Jerusalem, we can now say about our own city: *For the city has become to us as a terebinth stripped of leaves, and a garden having no water* (Is 1.30). For just as a garden, when its irrigation fails, turns into a desert, with its trees bereft of leaves and fruit, so also has our city become. For help from above has abandoned her, and she stands as a desert, having become stripped of nearly all her inhabitants.

Nothing is sweeter than one's homeland, but nothing is more bitter now. For all flee as from a snare from the place that brought them forth. They desert her as they would a dungeon; they leap away from her as if out of a fire. When a house goes up in flames, not only its inhabitants rush away with great haste, seeking to escape with nothing but their bare bodies, but those in the neighboring houses do so also. Likewise, with our city stricken with the threat of the expected wrath of the emperor descending as fire from above, everyone seeks to flee before it comes, to save themselves—if only with their own bare bodies.

Furthermore, our catastrophe has become an enigma. For there is flight without an enemy, a change of place without a battle, a captivity without a capture. We have not seen the fires of barbarians, or beheld the faces of warriors, and yet we are experiencing the sufferings of captives.

All around, the cities are learning of our calamity. For as they receive our refugees, they learn about the plague that has struck our city.

Yet I am not ashamed at this, and neither do I blush. Let everyone learn about our city's suffering, so that, in sympathizing with their mother, they may lift up to God their united voice across the whole earth, entreating with one desire the King of Heaven on behalf of the city that is the mother and nourisher of us all.

"A strange and new kind of siege"

Formerly our city was shaken by an earthquake, but now our very own souls are tottering. Then, the foundations of our houses shook; but now, the foundations of every heart quiver, and every day we all see death before our eyes. We constantly live with fear, enduring the torment of Cain[5]—something more pitiable than what is experienced by prison inmates, as we have been put under siege by a strange and new kind of siege, one far more fearsome than an ordinary siege.

[5]Cf. Gen 4.13–14.

For those who suffer a siege of enemy troops are only confined within the city walls, whereas for us it is even impossible to go to the forum, as we are closed up within the walls of our own homes. And just as those under a military siege are not safe upon venturing out beyond the city walls while the enemy is encamped there, so for many in our city it is not safe to venture out into the streets, or to appear openly at all, on account of those who are everywhere hunting for the guilty and the guiltless alike, seizing them in the midst of the forum and dragging them before the tribunal without proper procedures—only as chance directs.

For this reason, free men sit inside their homes, shackled up together with their servants, anxiously wondering who it is whom it might be safe to ask, "Who was seized today?" "Who was carried off?" "Who was punished?" "How so? In what manner?" They are living a life more pitiable than any kind of death, being compelled every day to mourn the calamities of others, while they tremble for their own safety and are in no better condition than the dead, in that they are already dead with fright.

If anyone who has no fear or agony desires to burst in upon the forum, he is immediately driven back to his own dwelling by the joyless scene he beholds, seeing scarcely one or two people, with their heads bent low, walking about with downcast eyes, where just a few days ago the multitudes were flowing like rivers through the city. But now, all this has been taken from us.

"Even the sun seems gloomy"

Just as when all the trees in a thick forest are cut down, the scene becomes joyless; and just as a head of hair having many patches of baldness—so our city, having its populace shrunken, and with only a few of its inhabitants appearing sporadically, has become joyless, casting a heavy gloom over everyone seeing all this. Not only the ground, but also the nature of the air is affected; and even the circle of the beams of the sun seems gloomy to me, and to be shining more dimly—not that the nature of the elements has changed, but that our own eyes, being clouded by the fog of torpor, are no longer able as before to perceive the rays of light clearly, or with the same calm disposition.

This is what the prophet of old bewailed in saying, *The sun shall go down at noonday, and the day will be dark* (Amos 8.9). This he said, not as though the sun would be hidden, or that the daylight would disappear, but because those who are engulfed with sorrow are not able to behold the noonday light, on account of the gloom of their anguish. This indeed has happened now.

And wherever anyone looks—whether at the ground, or at the walls, or at the columns of the city, or at his neighbors—he seems to see only night, and deep gloom: so full is everything of great melancholy!

"Silence everywhere, full of horror"

There is silence everywhere, full of horror. The city has become deserted, with that dear familiar hum of the multitude now quenched. It is as though everyone had descended beneath the earth, since such soundlessness has now seized the city. The people seem like stones; and just as if their mouths had been gagged by the tragedy, they maintain the most profound silence—as if enemies had come upon them and consumed them all at once by fire and sword!

Now is the right time to say, *Call for the wailing women, and the wise ones; let them come, and let them take up a great lament. Let your eyes flow with water, gushing with tears* (Jer 9.16–17). You hills, take up mourning! You mountains, lament! Let us call all of creation into sympathy with us for the evils that have befallen us.

This great city, head of all those under the eastern sky, is in danger of being ripped away from the civilized world! She who had so many children has now suddenly become childless, with no one coming to her aid! For he who has been so affronted has no one equal in honor to himself in the whole world, since the emperor is the summit and head of all the people on the earth.

Hence, let us flee unto the King above; let us call upon Him for help. For if we do not obtain the favor of Heaven, there is no consolation left for what has befallen us.

St John forces himself to speak

Here I would wish to bring my words to an end, since those whose souls are in anguish have no desire to extend their speaking to a great length. Just as a dense cloud blocks the rays of the sun and reflects their splendor back upwards, so the cloud of despondency, standing in front of our souls, does not allow free passage of our speech, but chokes it, forcing it to be stifled within.

This happens not only with those who speak, but also with those who hear. For just as despondency does not allow the words to flow forth freely from the soul of the speaker, so it also does not allow the words to sink into the minds of the listeners with their natural power.

Therefore also the Jews of old, slaving in mud and brick, had no readiness to listen to Moses speaking often about the great things concerning their deliverance. For their despondency made their minds inaccessible to his words, shutting down their sense of hearing.

Yes, I could have wished to bring my words to an end at this point. But then, I reflected that it is the nature of a cloud not only to block the rays of the sun, but that often the opposite happens: the sun, with its warmth continually beating upon the cloud, often wears it down, and breaking through the midst of it, suddenly shines forth, joyously meeting the gaze of those beholding the sight.

So this is what I expect to do today—to keep on speaking to your souls, so that with my words dwelling within you, I hope to burst through your cloud of despondency, so that our customary teaching may shine in your minds once again.

So open your souls to me! Give me your attention for a little while! Shake off this despondency! Let us return to our former custom, as we have always done: meeting here with gladness! Let us do so once again, while casting everything upon God. And this will contribute to our very deliverance from this calamity. For if He sees that His words are being heeded with great carefulness, and that our Christian philosophy is not undone by the difficulty of this moment, He will quickly come to our aid, transforming the present storm into something calm and good.

It is needful for the Christian to be different from unbelievers in this also—the bearing of all things nobly, and through hope for future good things, soaring above every attack of human evils. The believer stands on the Rock, and for this reason is untouched by the crashing of the waves. And if waves of temptation arise, they do not reach his feet, for he stands higher than any such plot.

So let us not fall down, beloved! We do not care about our own salvation as much as does God, the one who made us. We do not take as much care to avoid suffering affliction as does the one who gifted us with a soul and then gave us so many good things. So let us fly on the wings of these hopes, and let us listen to what is about to be spoken with our customary enthusiasm.

The Christians should have chastised the blasphemers in the city before the riot happened

Formerly I gave an extended oration to you, beloved,[6] and I saw all of you following along; no one was turning back while in the middle of the course. I return thanks to you for that enthusiasm, and I have received recompense for my labors.

But there was another recompense besides your attentiveness, which I asked of you at that time—perhaps you know what I am referring to. And what was that? That you should chastise and punish the blasphemers in our city, to restrain those who are insolent and violent against God. I do not think I gave that exhortation of my own accord; it was God who, foreseeing what was about to happen, put those words into my mind. For if we had dared to punish those men then, what has happened since then would not have happened.

How much better it would have been, if it had been necessary, to have suffered at the hands of such men, and even to have been adorned with a martyr's crown in trying to chasten and instruct them, than now to be in fright, to be trembling, to be expecting death because of their insurrection! Behold, the lawlessness was on the part of a

---

[6]He is most probably referring to the sermon he preached seven days before, which now stands as the first in the series, called *Homilies on the Statues*. In that sermon, he gave ten reasons why God sends or allows afflictions to come upon the saints—as if prophetically preparing the citizens of Antioch for the terrible riot that was to erupt four days later.

few, but the blame falls on us all! Behold how because of those few, everyone is now in fear; we are all enduring torment for what they dared to do! But if we had taken them and had cast them out of the city, and chastised them, correcting the wayward member, we would not be suffering from this present terror.

I know that from of old our city has been of a noble character. But lately, certain foreigners, men of mixed ancestry, pernicious, with blood on their hands, and with no regard for their own salvation, dared to do what they have done. Therefore I was always shouting out, and bearing witness without ceasing: "Let us punish the madness of these blasphemers; let us chastise their way of thinking; let us provide for their salvation. And even though we should die in so doing, it would be a deed that would bring us great reward. Let us not overlook how they have been affronting the Master whom we all have in common, for ignoring such things will bring forth great evil in our city."

I foretold these things, and now they have happened; and we are paying the penalty for that apathy. You overlooked the outrage that was done unto God, and now behold! He has permitted this outrage against the emperor, with the most extreme danger now hanging over us all, so that we might, by this terror, pay the price for that complacency.

So then! Was it in vain, was it to no purpose, that I foretold these things, continually imploring you, beloved? Nevertheless, no one did anything. But let something be done now! And with ourselves being chastened by this present calamity, let us hold in check the disorderly madness of these men. Let us close up their mouths, just as we close up fountains contaminated with poison. And let us turn them to a good path, so that the evils that have seized the city will be stopped.

The Church is not a theater, here to provide us delightful entertainment. Rather, it is needful for us to be here for spiritual benefit, gaining something great and satisfying before leaving. If we are won over only temporarily by the things that are spoken here, but then leave empty and barren of lasting benefit, we have gathered together in vain, to no purpose.

What benefit to me is this applause? And all this praise and cheering? Real praise for me is when you put into action all the things I say! I am blessed and exhilarated, not when you applaud me, but when you do with great enthusiasm whatever I say.

Let everyone, then, correct his neighbor; as it is said, *Edify one another* (1 Thess 5.11). For if we do not do this, the offenses of each one will bring widespread and unspeakable injury upon our city.

Behold, even though we ourselves are not aware of having any guilt from what has happened, we are frightened and terrified no less than the ones who perpetrated the calamity. We are all equally dreading lest the wrath of the emperor fall upon us all.

It's not enough for us to say in our defense, "I was not there, I did not see it, I did not have any part in what happened." For the emperor may well say, "For this reason you should be punished, even to be given over to the most extreme judgment, because you were not there, because you did not hold in check and restrain the rioters—and hence, because you risked no danger to defend my honor."

And such words as these we may hear from God Himself: "So you did not take part in what was audaciously and daringly done? I praise you for that. But you did not put a check to what was being done, and this is deserving of accusation."

So let us not continue to silently bear outrages and insults committed against God. For that one who buried his talent was called to account, not because of burying it—for he did return all of what he had been entrusted with—but because he did not increase it, he did not deposit his silver with the bankers, he did not use it to help others. In our present situation, we can say, he did not admonish, or counsel, or rebuke, or correct those evil rioters who were his neighbors. Because of this—coming back to the man with the talent—he was sent away, without any forgiveness, to those unbearable punishments.[7]

So now, even though you did not do so before, I strongly believe that you will accomplish this work of correction, and no longer overlook insults against God. For the things that have happened are sufficient, even if no one was given a warning, to convince men even greatly disposed to being negligent to exert themselves for their own safety.

[7]See Mt 25.14–30.

"Now it is time to lay before you the customary 'table' from St Paul"

Now it is time to lay before you the customary "table" from St Paul, by taking in hand the words of today's epistle reading and placing it before all of you for further consideration. What, then, was the text read today? *Exhort those who are wealthy in this age not to be high-minded* (1 Tim 6.17a). In saying, "those wealthy in this age," he is indicating that there are others who are rich in the things of the age to come. One such person was Lazarus, who was poor in regard to the things of this present life, but rich in the things of the future—not rich in gold and silver and other such things of material wealth, which are corruptible and ephemeral, but rich in those ineffable good things that *neither eye has seen, nor ear has heard, nor have entered into the heart of man* (1 Cor 2.9).

Teaching on wealth

This is true wealth, true opulence—when the possessions are flawless, and not subject to any change. The rich man who despised Lazarus did not have this kind of wealth; and hence, he became poorer than all men. So in the next life, when he sought to obtain but a drop of water, he was not deemed worthy to have even that—which shows to what extreme poverty he had fallen.

For this reason, Paul referred to those "wealthy in this present age," so that you might learn that when the present life comes to an end, all worldly opulence will be annihilated. It goes no further than the present life; it does not accompany those possessing it here and now when they are transferred into the next life.

And actually, their wealth often leaves them before their worldly demise. Paul shows this when he says, *Neither put your trust in uncertain riches* (1 Tim 6.17b). For nothing is so faithless as wealth, which I have often told you, and will never cease telling you. For it is an unfeeling runaway slave, having no fidelity; and if you should cast over it a myriad of chains, it would run off dragging the chains with it. For frequently, those possessing it have closed it up with bars and doors, stationing their servants as guards over it—and yet still, it has overpowered the guards, and has fled away, unbound, dragging along with it, as with a chain, those who were guarding it. So nothing more than this resulted from that assiduous guarding of the riches.

What could be more faithless than this? What can be more pitiable than those hastening after wealth? When men endeavor with all zeal to grasp this thing that is so frail and fleeting, they are not heeding the prophet when he says, Woe to those who *trust in their strength and boast in the multitude of their wealth* (Ps 48.6).

Tell me, why is this woe proclaimed?—*He heaps up treasures, and knows not for whom he shall gather them* (Ps 38.6). Indeed, the labor to acquire wealth is certain, but the enjoyment of it is not. For often it is for enemies that you toil and wear yourselves out—since often, after your decease, the inheritance of your wealth is enjoyed by those who have treated you unjustly, who have plotted against you in a myriad of ways.

Now it is worthy of inquiry why Paul did not say, "Exhort those who are wealthy in the present age not to be wealthy"; or "Exhort them to be poor"; or "Exhort them to be lacking things." Rather, he said, "Exhort them not to be high-minded." For he knew that the root, the underlying motivation, for gaining wealth is senseless folly;[8] and that if anyone knew how to be moderate, he would not in any way be zealous about acquiring wealth.

Tell me! Why do you lead around so many servants, parasites, flatterers, and every other kind of ostentation? Not out of necessity, surely, but only out of arrogance and folly, so that you might appear to be more important than other men.

Besides, Paul knew that wealth is not forbidden, if one uses it for that which is necessary. As I have told you, wine is not evil, but drunkenness is. So also wealth is not evil, but rapacity is, and lust for money.

A covetous person is one thing; a rich person is another. The covetous person is not rich, for he is in want of many things; and anyone needing many things can never be satisfied. The covetous one is a guard, not a master, of material goods. He is a slave, not a lord; for he would more easily surrender a portion of his own flesh than his buried gold. And just as if he were ordered and commanded not to touch what he has laid up for himself, yet still he will

---

[8]Greek: *aponoia*.

watch over it and keep it for himself, even while abstaining from touching it, as if it belonged to someone else.

And indeed, it does belong to another. For how can he call it his own when he feels he cannot even bestow it upon others, or give it to those in need, even if he endures a myriad of punishments for not doing so? How does he possess those things that he does not have free control over, and which he does not enjoy?

Besides this, Paul customarily does not command everyone to do everything that is possible, for he makes allowance for the weakness of his hearers, just as Christ did. For when that rich man approached Him, and asked about eternal life, He did not say, "Go, and sell your possessions." Rather, putting that aside, He spoke to him of other commandments. And after that, when the man challenged Him, saying, *What, then, do I lack?* neither even then did He simply say, "Sell your possessions," but rather, *If you wish to be perfect, go, sell your possessions* (Mt 19.20). Hence, He was saying, in effect, "I leave it for you to decide; I make you master over your power to choose; I do not lay upon you any necessity."

Therefore, Paul never spoke to the rich about becoming poor, but about having humility, on account of the weakness of his listeners, and knowing well that if he could get them to be moderate, to be delivered from senselessness, he could quickly deliver them from their zeal for acquiring wealth.

Furthermore, upon warning them about being high-minded, he taught them how to avoid being that way.

And what was this? That they should ponder the nature of wealth—how unsteady and faithless it is! Therefore, he adds, *Neither place your hope in uncertain riches*. For the truly wealthy man is not the one possessing much, but rather the one giving much.

The wealth of Abraham

Abraham was wealthy, but not covetous; he did not look around at anyone else's house, neither did he get worked up over someone else's possessions. Rather, going forth, he looked around for where there might be a stranger, or a poor man, in order that he might alleviate the poverty of the poor man and hospitably receive the traveler. He did not cover his roof with gold, but pitching his tent by the oak tree, he was content with the shade of its leaves.

Yet so splendid was the lodging he could provide that angels were not ashamed to tarry with him.[9] For they were not seeking the most illustrious dwelling, but virtue of soul. This is what is necessary for us to emulate, beloved. So let us bestow what we have upon those in need.

The lodging Abraham offered was rustic, yet it was more splendid than the halls of kings. No king has ever given hospitality to angels; yet the one sitting under that oak tree, and having pitched a tent there, was deemed worthy of that honor, though he was not so honored on account of the simplicity of his dwelling. Rather, he enjoyed that gift because of the greatness of his soul, and the wealth deposited therein.

[9]See Gen 18.1–15.

Our splendid houses are of no help now

So let us adorn, not our houses, but instead of them, our own souls. For how is it not shameful and in vain and to no purpose to cover the walls of our house with marble when we neglect to clothe Christ as he goes around naked?[10] Of what profit is your house to you, O man? For will you take it with you when you depart from this life? Indeed, you will not be taking it with you when you depart; but you will certainly be taking your soul!

Behold now, how great this danger is that has overtaken us! Let our houses stand by us! Let them deliver us from the threatened peril! But they cannot! You yourselves are witnesses of that, since you are leaving them empty and fleeing to the desert, fearing staying in them as if they were snares and traps.

Let your riches help you now! But there is no time for them to do so. So then, if the power of riches counts for so little before the wrath of a man, how much more will that be the case before the inevitable divine tribunal! If it is but a man who is now provoked and offended, and gold is of no benefit to us, how much more will the power of gold be weak then, when God is angered—He who has no need of gold!

We should build houses simply in order to live in them—not to make a grand display! Whatever is beyond our needs is superfluous and useless. If you put on a sandal that is bigger than your foot, you will not be able to bear it, for it will become a hindrance to your stride. So

[10]See Mt 25.31–46.

also a house that is bigger than what is necessary is an impediment on your journey to Heaven.

Do you wish to build large and splendid houses? I do not forbid you—but not here on the earth! Rather, build your tabernacles in Heaven, so that you may be truly able to give hospitality to others—for those tabernacles will never fall apart.

The harried rich, the unencumbered poor

Why are you so in turmoil over fleeting things, which must all be eventually left here anyway? Nothing is more slippery than wealth, which today is with you, and tomorrow is against you. For it arms the eyes of the envious everywhere. It is a hostile comrade, a domestic enemy. You are witnesses—how those with great possessions are always seeking to conceal and hide their wealth, so that even now our wealth makes the present danger more unbearable for us.

You see how the poor are girded for action, unencumbered and freed from distractions, prepared for anything that might happen, while the rich are harried with concerns, looking all about, seeking a place to bury their gold, or someone with whom to entrust it.

Entrust your riches to Christ

Why, O man, do you seek among your fellow slaves someone to entrust it with? For Christ stands ready to receive and keep your riches for you—and not only to keep them, but to increase them, and to return them with much interest gained. No one can seize your wealth out of His hands. And not only does He keep and protect your riches, but He relieves you from the perils associated with keeping them yourselves.

And furthermore, among men, those who keep your goods for you think that they are doing you a favor. But with Christ it is the opposite. For He is not bestowing a favor on you when you entrust your possessions to Him; rather, He receives your goods as a favor to Him and to those whom He will benefit through them. And He does not demand a recompense from you as men do; rather, He gives you a recompense!

So then! What defense are we entitled to claim, what excuse can we make, when we "run past" the one who is truly able to keep our goods, who is thankful for the trust, and who gives in return great and unspeakable rewards, and instead of that heavenly guardianship we entrust our goods into the keeping of weak men, who think they are granting us a favor, and only return to us what we have entrusted to them?

Are you not a stranger and a sojourner in regard to the things of this life? You have a fatherland in the heavens! So transfer your goods there, so that instead of enjoying those things here, you may enjoy your spiritual reward here and now! For one who is nourished with benevolent hopes, and has boldness about future things, already tastes the things of the future Kingdom here and now.

Customarily, nothing so renews a soul and makes a man better, than having a good hope of things to come.

And if you transfer your wealth there, you will provide your soul with suitable leisure. For those who expend all their zeal on adorning their houses, rich as they may be outwardly, are negligent about inner things, allowing their souls to abide in desolation and squalor, full of spiders' webs. But if they are indifferent about outward things, and eagerly devote all their attention to the disposition of their mind and heart, adorning them in every way, then the souls of such people will become lodging places for Christ.

Having Christ dwelling within one's soul! What could ever be more blessed than that?

Do you wish to be wealthy? Have God as your friend, and you will be overflowing with abundance more than anyone else!

A proper perspective on wealth

Do you wish to be wealthy? Do not be high-minded. This rule is fitting not only regarding things of the future, but also regarding present things. For there is no one who is an object of envy as much as the wealthy man. But when senseless folly[11] is added, the precipice becomes twofold, and the war becomes fiercer on all sides.

But when you know how to be moderate, you undercut by your humility the tyranny of jealousy, and with safety you can possess whatever you have. For such is the nature of virtue that it is of profit not only in regard to things of the future, but already here and now it brings us rewards.

[11]Greek: *aponoia*.

Let us not, then, be high-minded regarding our wealth, or anything else whatsoever. For if even regarding spiritual things the one who is high-minded is fallen and undone, much more is this so regarding carnal things. Let us be mindful of our human nature; let us recollect and ponder upon our sins; let us understand who we are. This will suffice to be the foundation for complete humility.

Do not tell me, "I have laid up the revenues of such and such number of years, myriads of talents of gold, gains that are increasing every day." Say whatever you will, you will be speaking vainly and to no purpose. For often, in one hour, even in one short moment of time, everything is whisked out of the house, like light dust when a wind rushes down from above.

Our life is full of examples like this, and the Scriptures are full of such lessons. He who is rich today is poor tomorrow. Therefore I have often smiled when reading wills saying, "Let a certain person have ownership of my fields, or my house; and let another have the use thereof." For we all only have the use of things; no one really has ownership of anything. Even if our wealth remains with us unchanged throughout our whole lifetime, in the end we must transfer it to others, whether willingly or unwillingly. After having had only temporary enjoyment of it, we will depart to the next life destitute and empty of any degree of ownership of it.

So it is evident that those who have in any sense possessed wealth are only those who despise it, deriding the enjoyment of it; and so, casting it away from themselves, they bestow it upon the poor, which is its proper use. In this way such a person departs to the next life having ownership of his goods, which even death does not rob him of, for at that time he receives back all that he gave away in this life, and much more besides—all of which will help him especially on the Day of Judgment, when all of us will be called to account for the deeds we have done.

So if anyone wishes to have possessions, and to have the use of them as well as the ownership of them, let him extricate himself from them all. And anyway, anyone not doing this will be separated from his goods at his death. Indeed, often even before death one loses his possessions, living as we do in the midst of dangers and innumerable evils.

This is not the only danger—that a reversal of fortune may occur suddenly—but also that the wealthy person becomes most inexperienced in enduring poverty. But not so with the poor person, for he does not put his confidence in gold and silver, which are lifeless matter, but *in God, who provides all things abundantly* (1 Tim 6.17c). Rather than the one who is poor, it is the rich person who stands in uncertainty, experiencing as he does frequent and various changes of fortune.

God's abundant liberality of needful things

So what does it mean, *Who provides us with all things abundantly to enjoy* (1 Tim 6.17c)? God gives everything with liberality, things that are much more necessary than riches—such as air, water, fire, the sun, and all such things. For the wealthy person cannot say that he enjoys more of the sun's rays than the poor person does; and he cannot say that he breathes in the air more plentifully. For these things are offered equally to all.

Why is it, one may ask, that God has made the greater and more needful things common to us all, while making the lesser things not common for all—things such as money. Why is this? In order that our life[12] might be well-disciplined, and that we might have a training ground for virtue. If needful things were not held in common, the rich, with their customary greediness, might well strangle the poor. For if they do this for the sake of gaining money, how much more would they do so with respect to necessary things? And also, if money were held in common, and offered to everyone equally, the occasion for almsgiving, the opportunity for expressing kindliness,[13] would be taken away.

So that we may live securely, then, the sources of our life have been made common. And in order for us to have the opportunity to gain crowns and good report, money has not been made common, so that by hating covetousness and pursuing righteousness, by giving freely to those in need, we may in these ways gain a certain comfort and relief from our sins.

God has made you rich—so why do you make yourself poor? He has made you rich, so that you might help the needy, so that you might be loosed from your sins through your benevolence to others. He has given you

---

[12]Greek: *zōēs*.
[13]Greek: *philophrosynēs*.

money, not that you would shut it up unto yourself for your destruction, but that you would pour it out for your salvation.

The uncertainty and instability of riches

Therefore He has also made the possession of riches uncertain and unstable, so that because of this your mania for them might be slackened in intensity. For if those possessing wealth, even while they cannot have full confidence in it, and while they behold the many machinations that are born from it, are nevertheless on fire with desire to have it, if the characteristics of firmness and dependability had been added to it, whom would they have spared? Whom would they have refrained from ravaging? What widows? What orphans? What poor folk?

So let us not consider wealth to be a great good. What is a great good is not possessing money, but possessing the fear of God and every form of piety.

Prayer, not riches, moves God

Behold now, if there were someone righteous in our midst having great boldness with God, even if he were the poorest of all men, he would be able to free us from the present fearsome dangers. It would be enough for him to stretch out his hands towards Heaven and call upon God, and the present cloud overhanging us would pass away!

There is such a great amount of gold stored up in this city, and yet it is more worthless than clay to deliver us from the impending evils. And not only in a time of danger like this, but also if illness strikes, if death approaches, if any other such thing occurs, the impotence of possessions to help us is fully proven, since they have no comfort to offer in such times.

Many advantages of poverty, if it is borne wisely

There is one way in which wealth seems to have an advantage over poverty—that it provides luxury every day, and supplies an abundance of pleasure at banquets. This, however, may also be seen at the table of the poor, where they enjoy greater pleasure than do all those who are wealthy. Do not marvel at this! Do not think what I am saying is an enigma. For I will make the matter clear to you through an examination of the facts.

You know, certainly, and you all would agree, that at banquets it is not the nature of the gourmet foods that usually gives pleasure, but rather this depends on the condition and disposition of those feasting upon them. As an example of what I am saying, when anyone approaches the table hungry, whatever he eats, even if it's the most ordinary of foods, will taste better than any sauce, or condiment, or a myriad of exquisite dishes. But the one who does not wait to be hungry—who does not wait until necessity makes him eat (as is often the case with the wealthy)—when he comes to the table, even though he finds sumptuous dishes spread before him, he will have no pleasure in them, since his appetite has not been previously stimulated.

And that you may learn that this is indeed the way things are, even though you all are witnesses of this already, listen to what the Scriptures say about it: *The full soul scorns the honeycomb, but to the hungry soul, even bitter things appear sweet* (Prov 27.7). What can be sweeter than honey, or a honeycomb? Yet he says it is not sweet to one who is not hungry. And what can be more unpleasurable than bitter things? Yet to those who are poverty-stricken, they are sweet.

The poor come to their meals with need, with hunger, while the rich do not wait for that—this is evident to everyone. Hence, they do not reap the fruit of genuine and undiluted pleasure.

This is the case not only with food, but the same thing also occurs with drink, as anyone can see. And as in the first case hunger is the source of the pleasure more than the nature of the food, so in this second case—thirst usually makes the drink sweeter, even if what is drunk is only water.

This is what the Prophet [David] made known when he said, *With honey out of the rock He satisfied them* (Ps 80.16). Yet we do not read anywhere in the Scriptures that Moses brought honey out of a rock; rather, in the account about him we read of rivers, and waters, and cool streams.

What, then, do those words mean? For the Scriptures never lie. Since, then, those Hebrews were so exhausted and parched with thirst, and then found the streams of water to be so cooling, the Psalmist, wishing to indicate the pleasure that drink gave them, called the water "honey"—not as though its nature had changed into honey, but because the condition of those who drank it made the water seem sweet like honey.

So do you understand how the condition of those who are athirst often makes their drink sweet? Often, many of the poor, when wearied and distressed, and afflicted with thirst, have partaken of such streams of water with the pleasure I have spoken of; while the rich, even if drinking the sweetest wine, fragrant with the scent of flowers, having every perfection that wine can have, experience no such cheer in it.

The same thing is true, as anyone can see, regarding sleep. For sleep is usually not made nearly as sweet and pleasant by a soft couch, or a bed overlaid with silver, or by the quietness of the home, or by any other such thing, as by labors and weariness and the need for sleep, and the drowsiness that occurs upon lying down on one's bed in such a state.

An assertion of the Scriptures bears witness to this, even before one's experience of this fact. For Solomon, who spent his life in luxury, desired to make this clear when he said, *Sweet is the sleep of the servant, whether he eats little or much* (Eccl 5.11a). And why does he add, "whether he eats little or much"? Because both of these things, both a lack and an excess of food, usually result in sleeplessness—the one by withering the body, stiffening the eyelids, not allowing them to be closed, and the other by straitening and restricting one's breathing, and producing many pains. But so powerful is the comfort coming from labors that even if either of these things befall him, the servant is able to sleep. Since all the day long servants serve their masters, running about here and there, being knocked around, getting worn out, and scarcely having a chance to breathe, they receive the pleasure of sleep as a sufficient reward for all their labors and pains.

Thus it happened, through the work of the God who loves mankind, that the pleasures of sound sleep are not to be purchased with gold and silver, but with labors and hard toil, and necessity, and all the forms of Christian philosophizing. But it is not like this with the rich; for often, while lying on their beds, they are sleepless all night long, not enjoying that pleasure even despite their many contrivances to help them do so. But the poor man, when released from his daily labors, with his limbs exhausted, almost before he falls into bed, immediately receives sweet and genuine sleep, gaining this as no little reward for his just labors.

Since, therefore, the poor man sleeps, and drinks, and eats with more pleasure than the rich man, what further worth does wealth have, now that we see how it lacks the very advantages over poverty that it seemed to have?

For this reason also, God in the beginning yoked labor to man—not to punish him, or to torment him, but to instruct him, to make him wise. When Adam lived without labor in Paradise, he fell from there; but when the Apostle Paul, having worked hard and labored mightily, saying, *in labors and travail, working night and day* (2 Cor 11.27), then he was taken up into Paradise, and even ascended to the third Heaven!

Let us not, therefore, think badly of labor, neither let us despise work, since besides the Kingdom of Heaven, we receive the very greatest recompense from it, even reaping pleasure from it—and not pleasure only, but also something much greater than pleasure: the purest health. In addition to the general unpleasantness that is typical of the life of the rich, many diseases also attack them; while the poor are generally freed from the hands of physicians. And if at times they fall into sickness, they quickly recover themselves, for they are free from all weakness and softness, having soundness of body.

For those who bear it wisely,[14] poverty is a great possession, a treasure that cannot be stolen, the strongest staff, a possession that cannot be harmed, a safe place that cannot be plotted against. One may say that the poor man is defrauded and oppressed. But the rich man is more likely to be plotted against. The poor man may be despised and insulted, but the rich man is subject to being envied. The poor man is not as easily assaulted as the rich man is, for the rich man's wealth makes him vulnerable on every side to a myriad of machinations of the devil, as well as the fact that he is a servant to everyone because of the far-reaching extent of his affairs. Standing in need of many things, he is compelled to flatter many people, and to serve them with much servility.

---

14 Lit. "philosophically" (*philosophōs*).

But the poor man, if he knows how to be spiritually astute,[15] is not so vulnerable to attack even by the devil himself. Thus Job, strong as he was before, when he lost everything, he became stronger still, and gained a brilliant victory over the devil.

Dealing with insults philosophically

Besides this, the poor man cannot be outraged by insults, if he knows how to be philosophical. For what I said about pleasure at a banquet—that it comes not from the costly provision of elegant foods, but from the condition and disposition of those eating there—so, I say, it's the same with insults. For an insult either takes hold or dissipates, depending on the disposition of the one being insulted, rather than on that of the one doing the insulting.

For example: someone insults you with many words either repeatable or unrepeatable. But if you laugh at the insult, if you do not let in the words, if you stand above the blow, you are not actually insulted. For if we have a body like steel, and are attacked on all sides by a myriad of arrows, we would not even be pricked by the darts.

On the other hand, if we are weak, insults do become real and wound us, not because of the madness[16] of the one launching the attack, but because of our inner weakness. But if we know how to be truly wise,[17] it will be impossible for us to be insulted, or to suffer any deep sorrow.

15 Lit. "to philosophize" (*philosophein*).
16 Greek: *mania*.
17 Lit. "to philosophize" (*philosophein*).

It may be that someone tries to insult you; but if you do not let it affect you, have you really been hurt? Hence, you have not really been insulted; rather, you have delivered the blow! For when the one insulting and reviling you sees that his blows have not affected you, he himself is more greatly stung. For when those being insulted remain silent, the blow turns backward on its own accord, and recoils upon the one who launched the dart.

"So let us abound in Christian philosophy"

So let us abound in Christian philosophy in all things, my beloved, and poverty will not be able to do us any harm. Rather, it will benefit us greatly, rendering us more illustrious, and wealthier than all the rich. For tell me, who was poorer than Elijah? Yet for this very reason he surpassed all the wealthy, in that he was so poor, and because he chose this poverty out of the riches of his own mind and heart. For since he considered the accumulation of all riches to be beneath greatness of soul, and not worthy of spiritual wisdom, therefore he welcomed this degree of poverty.

Certainly, if he had considered present things to be great, he would not have possessed only a mantle. For indeed, he had so much contempt for the vanity of all present things, regarding gold as cast-off clay, that he possessed nothing more than that covering for his body. Yet even the king [Ahab] had need of that poor man; and he who owned much gold hung upon the words of him who owned only a sheepskin.[18] Thus was the sheepskin more illustrious than the king's purple, and the cave of the just man was more splendid than the halls of kings.

So when he went up to Heaven, he left nothing else to his disciple except that sheepskin, saying, "With this I fought against the devil; so take it, and it alone, and be armed against him!" For having no possessions in itself is a powerful weapon, an unassailable safe place, an unshakeable fortress.

Elisha received the sheepskin as the greatest inheritance; and truly it was a great inheritance, more precious than all gold. From then on, Elijah was a two-fold person—an Elijah on high, and an Elijah [in Elisha] here below!

I know you all consider Elijah, that righteous one, to be blessed, and each of you would desire to be that one. What, then, if I show you that all those among us who have been initiated into the Mysteries of Baptism and the Eucharist have received something far greater than he did? For Elijah, when he ascended on high, left a sheepskin mantle to his disciple; but the Son of God, upon ascending on high, left us His own Flesh! Elijah indeed was stripped of his cloak when he went up; but Christ, in leaving His Flesh here [in the Eucharist], still retained it as He ascended into Heaven.

"Let us not, then, be cast down"

Let us not, then, be cast down; let us not lament; let us not fear the difficulty of this present moment! For He who

[18]See 3 Kingdoms LXX (1 Kgs) 18.

did not refuse to pour out His very Blood for all mankind, giving us His Flesh and his Blood to partake of—what will He not refuse to do for our present deliverance?

Having confidence, therefore, in these hopes, let us beseech Him continually. Let us be earnest in our prayers and supplications, while being meticulously careful in cultivating every other virtue, so that we may escape from the danger that now hangs over us, and attain the future good things.

May we all be worthy of this—by the grace and love for mankind of our Lord Jesus Christ, through whom and with whom be glory to the Father, together with the Holy Spirit, now and ever, and unto ages of ages. Amen.[19]

[19]St John permanently won the hearts of the people of Antioch through the love, wisdom, and encouragement that he poured forth to them in the sermons that he preached during this most penitential of all Great Lents in that city. As his biographer J. N. D. Kelly writes, "With even pagans flocking to hear them, these homilies amply confirmed John's position as Antioch's leading preacher. From now on, as a German scholar [O. Bardenhewer] well expressed it, he had the hearts and ears of the entire population wide open for him." J. N. D. Kelly, *Golden Mouth: The Story of John Chrysostom: Ascetic, Preacher, Bishop* (Grand Rapids, MI: Baker Books, 1995), 82.

Thankfully, through the people's myriad of intercessions to God for mercy, and through the help of the elderly Archbishop Flavian, who traveled all the way to Constantinople to personally intercede before Emperor Theodosius the Great, the emperor did show mercy. He rescinded the punitive measures he had taken against the city, he reaffirmed imperial favor for the city, and he restored it to its honorary position as the leading city in Syria.

Homily after the Earthquake

A note on the text

The two great cities in which St John Chrysostom lived and ministered—Antioch and Constantinople—lie on fault lines, so both cities are prone to earthquakes. We have two sermons given by St John Chrysostom after earthquakes that shook Antioch—the first, in 388, and the second, at the end of 395 or the beginning of 396. This is a translation of the second of these two homilies.

Apparently St John had been ill for some time and absent from the pulpit until he was able to preach on the preceding day. He is still rejoicing to be back with his beloved flock, and especially to be able to console them further after the earthquake. As he says to them poignantly and powerfully, "Up until yesterday, I was fixed in my bed; but God did not permit that I should be entirely ruined by this famine. For just as it is a famine for you not to hear, so it is a famine for me not to speak."

And what he expresses most in this homily is thankfulness for how his flock has kept all-night vigils for a few nights in a row, beginning when the earthquake—which lasted two days—started, and continuing even after it stopped. For he remarks with joy and amazement that they came to church to hear him preach still "dripping with sweat" from keeping vigil all night.

Further, he is convinced that the earthquake stopped because of their all-night prayer and psalmody, and their processions through the city streets. As he says, "I rejoice, not that the city is still standing, but because it was through your prayers that it still stands, and that your psalmody became its foundations." And furthermore, he tells them: "You accomplished a great all-night vigil, and you purified the entire city with the steps of your holy feet, having measured out the marketplace with your walking about it. You have even made the air holy, for the air becomes holy through the singing of psalms."

He also speaks rapturously of the benefit of the earthquake for the city's inhabitants, that it brought them so quickly to deep repentance and wonderful amendment of life:

> How were you harmed by being upset for a little while? You became angels instead of men. You transferred yourselves to Heaven—if not in place, yet in your way of life. … You cast out envy, you got free of your slavish passions, you implanted virtue, you spent the whole night in holy vigils with good

strength, much love, and an eager disposition….
No one abuses his neighbor, no one goes off to
satanic "festivals." Households are pure, the marketplace has been cleansed. Evening arrives, and
no longer are there youths singing the songs of the
theater. Still there are songs being sung, but not
of licentiousness—rather, they are songs of righteousness.

Here are St John's words of encouragement, praise, and
thanksgiving for his dear flock, whom he describes thus:
"You, my congregation, are my crown! And just one of
you listeners is worth the whole city."

Homily after the Earthquake[1]

Even if my infirmity prevented me from joining with you in the spiritual chorus before yesterday, yet the labor of your journey did not prevent you from being here. And even if your effort led you here dripping with sweat, yet the teaching of the Word transformed my infirmity into health; and through the chanting of the Psalms, your pain was eased.

Therefore, even though I was ill, I did not bind my tongue in silence; and neither did you, though you were wearied, remove yourselves from hearing my discourse. And as soon as the word shone forth, your pains retreated; as soon as the teaching became manifest, your weariness

[1]PG 50:713–16; Modern Greek: *Iōannou tou Chrysostomou Erga*, 3:79–82.

fled away. For illness and pain are of the body, while spiritual teaching is for the right-ordering and healing of the soul. And however much the soul is better than the body, by that much the right-ordering of the soul is more valuable than physical health.

And so, not only with infirmity hindering me, but with a myriad of other obstacles happening also, still I did not withdraw from being intertwined in your love[2] yesterday. And today I have not been deprived of this beautiful feast.

Up until yesterday, I was fixed in my bed; but God did not permit that I should be entirely ruined by this famine. For just as it is a famine for you not to hear, so it is a famine for me not to speak. Just as a mother, though she may often be sick, prefers that her breast be stretched by her child rather than see the child waste away because of hunger, may my body also be stretched! For who would not gladly pour out his blood for you—you who are so zealous in godliness and watchfulness, and who have shown forth such repentance in a small moment of time?[3]

You do not know the difference between day and night, as you make them both day—not by transforming the elements, but by illumining the night with your vigils. Your nights are sleepless; the tyranny of sleep has been destroyed. For your yearning[4] for Christ has conquered the weakness of your nature. You ceased from being human in your bodies, so to speak, by imitating the

2 Greek: *agapē*.
3 Greek: *kairou*.
4 Greek: *pothos*.

heavenly powers, showing forth sleeplessness, and earnest fasting, and such great labor because of your journey—labor that nature demanded, even as it was still possible to choose rest.

This is the fruit, the benefit, of the fears generated by the earthquake—benefit that will never be used up, benefit that makes the poor more well-off and enriches the wealthy. The earthquake did not know either poverty or wealth; it came and leveled the unevenness of worldly circumstance.

Where now are those enveloped in silken garments? Where is the gold? All these things have gone away, torn apart more easily than a spider's web, disappearing more quickly than springtime flowers.

But since I see that your minds are prepared, I wish to lay out for you a more richly laden table. I see your bodies worn down, but your soul renewed. The fountains of sweat are many, but they wipe the conscience clean. And if athletes drip with blood to win a crown of laurel leaves that is given today and withered tomorrow, how much more is it necessary for you who enter the struggle for righteous deeds not to falter in the labor for virtue, and not to grow soft.

You, my congregation, are my crown! And just one of you listeners is worth the whole city.

Some people have "honored" bowls mixed with wine and water,[5] others have gathered at satanic "festivals," and

---

[5] At banquets, wine would be poured into bowls, and then water would be added.

others have prepared sumptuous tables. But you accomplished a great all-night vigil, and you purified the entire city with the steps of your holy feet, having measured out the marketplace with your walking about it. You have even made the air holy, for the air becomes holy through the singing of psalms—as today you heard God saying to Moses, *The place where you are standing is holy* (Ex 3.5).

You sanctified the ground, the marketplace; you made our whole city a church. Just as a great river, swollen into a mighty torrent, overturns everything in its path, so the spiritual torrent, the river of God that gladdens the city of God,[6] cleanses away the mire of impiety with its overflowing waters.

Now no one is licentious—or if he is licentious, he is being changed. He hears the voice of the psalmody, and his mind is transformed; the melody enters in, and his impiety is changed, and he flees from the passion of greediness.

And even if he does not flee, just as beasts in winter lie torpid in their dens, so his lascivious mind is buried in the earth. And just as serpents, when cold stiffens their bodies, go down below the ground, so too these passions, servile and slavish, are hidden as if in an abyss.

Of course, those harboring such things are ashamed; yet even though their passions are still within, they are deadened. And instead of winter, it is your melody that comes to them; and when the sound of it comes into the hearing of the greedy man, even if he does not cast out the passion, at least it has died within him. And when its

[6]See Ps 45.4.

sound comes into the hearing of the licentious and arrogant man, even if it does not kill the lasciviousness and haughtiness, it buries those passions within him. So as we see, it's not a small matter *not* to speak out boldly against wickedness.

I said yesterday that great is the fruit of the earthquake. Do you see the Lord's love for mankind[7] in shaking the city and making your minds firm? In rocking the foundations, and making your thoughts steadfast? In cracking the city, and strengthening your powers of discernment?

Consider His love for mankind. He shook the city for a little while, but He makes us strong constantly. The earthquake lasted for two days; let piety endure for all time. You were distressed for a little while, but now you are rooted continuously. For I well know that it was from your fear of God that your piety took root. And if there is respite, the fruit remains.

No longer are the thorn bushes choking us; no longer is an overwhelming rain washing us away. That fear cultivated you well; it became an ally of my words. I am silent, and the foundations speak out; I am quiet, and the earthquake brings forth a sound more piercing than a trumpet, saying these things: *The Lord is compassionate and merciful, long-suffering and plenteous in mercy* (Ps 102.8); and, "I was with you, not to cast you down, but to invigorate you."

These things the earthquake says, sending forth its voice: "I frightened you, not to make you despair, but to

---

[7]Greek: *philanthrōpian.*

make your way of life more exact. Pay precise attention to my words. For when the sermon was ineffectual, help cried out; when the teaching weakened, fear fought as an ally. I came bringing my discourse to you for a short while, doing my part. Now I give you over to the sermon, having straitened you, so that the sermon may have effect. Finding stones, and thorn bushes growing, I made the land clean, so that the sermon may scatter its seeds with a lavish hand."

How were you harmed by being upset for a little while? You became angels instead of men. You transferred yourselves to Heaven—if not in place, yet in your way of life.[8] And that I do not say these things to flatter you, the facts bear witness. For in what way did you fall short regarding my sermon on repentance? You cast out envy, you got free of your slavish passions; you implanted virtue; you spent the whole night in holy vigils with good strength, much love,[9] and an eager disposition.

Now no one remembers collecting interest, no one speaks about greediness. And not only are your hands without sin, but also your tongue is delivered from reviling and lawlessness. No one abuses his neighbor, no one goes off to satanic "festivals." Households are pure, the marketplace has been cleansed. Evening arrives, and no longer are there youths singing the songs of the theater.

Still there are songs being sung, but not of licentiousness—rather, they are songs of righteousness. And in the

[8] A play on words in Greek: *mē tō topō, alla tō tropō.*
[9] Greek: *agapē.*

marketplace hymnody is heard, and among those sitting at home, one sings psalms and another sings other hymns of the Church. Night arrives, and all are in church—the waveless harbor, the place that has been delivered from turmoil.

I was thinking that after one or two days, sleeplessness would have overcome your bodies. But by however much your sleeplessness is taxing you, by that much your desire[10] increases. Those singing psalms to you were worn out, while you were renewed; the chanters grew weak, while you became strong.

Tell me, where now are the wealthy? Let them learn the Christian philosophy of the poor. For they sleep, but the poor do not even sleep on the ground; rather, they bend their knees, following the example of Paul and Silas. And while they sang psalms and shook open the prison,[11] you sang psalms and kept the shaking city standing.

The outcomes were contrary to each other, yet they both were for the glory of God. For He shook the prison in order to shake the minds of the disbelieving, to dislodge the jailor, to proclaim the Word of God; while you sang psalms in order to undo God's anger and make the city stand.

The two outcomes were arranged differently, but nevertheless I rejoice, not that the city is still standing, but because it was through your prayers that it still stands, and that your psalmody became its foundations. His wrath

[10]Greek: *pothos*.
[11]Acts 16.25–26.

from above, your voice from below: your voice, sent from below, checked the wrath flowing from above.

The heavens were opened, and a judgment was brought down—the sharpened sword. The wrath appeared inevitable, about to knock the city to the ground. Yet we had need of nothing except repentance, tears, and groaning; and everything was averted.

God appeared, and we ourselves dissolved His wrath. One would not be mistaken in calling you the caretakers and saviors of the city.

Where were the rulers? Where were the great ones of the city? Truly you are the towers, the walls, the security of the city. For they, by their own wickedness, allowed the city to deteriorate; while you, by your own virtue, made the city to stand firm.

If someone should be asked why the city was shaken, even if he does not admit it, it is agreed that this happened because of sins—because of acts of greediness, and injustice, and lawlessness, and arrogance, and illicit pleasure, and deceit. And who were responsible for all of this? The rich.

And if someone should be asked why the city still stood firm, it is agreed that this happened because of psalmody, and prayers, and vigils. And who was responsible for all of that? The poor.

The city was shaken because of the wealthy; it still stands because of you. Hence, you have become its caretakers and saviors.

But let us bring our discourse to an end here, while we all remain in our vigils and psalmody, sending up glory to the Father, and to the Son, and to the Holy Spirit, now and ever, and unto ages of ages. Amen.

First Homily on Eutropius

Early in 399, Eutropius, a wily and exceedingly ambitious court eunuch, had attained the highest position in the imperial government, that of consul; he was the only eunuch ever to reach such heights. He was also the grand chamberlain in the imperial court in Constantinople. He was fabulously wealthy, but apparently much of that wealth was acquired through extortion in various ways.

He had arranged the marriage of Emperor Arcadius with Eudoxia, a Germanic princess, in 395, and he had such influence with the imperial couple that he was considered to be the most powerful person in the Eastern Roman Empire. Having such influence over the quite weak Emperor Arcadius, it is held that it was most likely he who suggested that John, the great preacher of Antioch, should succeed Nectarius, who had died near the end of 397, as archbishop of Constantinople.

Later in 399, Eutropius suddenly fell out of favor with Empress Eudoxia, who had been protecting him from mounting popular opposition against him. When imperial guards were sent to arrest him, he managed to flee to the leading church of the city, Hagia Sophia, where St John was the main preacher, and where he had his living quarters. Once inside the church, the panic-stricken man ran up and seized the altar, and clung to it for dear life.

This is the setting for the following sermon preached by Chrysostom on the day after Eutropius fled into the church, as he was again clinging to the altar. Very much to St John's credit, and as a wonderful testimony to his deep and Christ-filled magnanimity, he allowed Eutropius to stay in the cathedral as a place of refuge from the authorities. This is all the more remarkable in that Eutropius had done some things that were harmful to the Church, as we can tell from John referring in this sermon to "the Church that you made war against."

Ironically, one of the things Eutropius had done against the Church was restricting her right to provide sanctuary to those fleeing there. But not only does St John forgive the man, we also we see in this sermon the archbishop urging his flock to do the same, in spite of all the man's animosity and misdeeds.

At the beginning of this homily, St John addresses Eutropius directly—not with any scorn or triumphalism, but with tremendous compassion and sympathy. And yes, consummate teacher and preacher that he is, he sees this as an excellent opportunity to teach his flock about the ephemeral nature of everything in this world.

The entire sermon highlights the vast loving mercy of the Church for all who come to her. It is a great example to us of Christian forgiveness of, and love for, enemies, as exemplified by a hierarch who leads by humbly serving his own people and even his enemies.

Shortly after this sermon was preached, mercy was indeed shown to the disgraced consul and grand chamberlain. Instead of being immediately tried and executed, he was exiled to Cyprus. Nevertheless, shortly thereafter, Eutropius was recalled from exile, tried, found guilty of high treason, and beheaded in Chalcedon, a suburb of Constantinople.

First Homily on Eutropius[1]

Vanity of vanities! All is vanity! (Eccl 1.2) It is always appropriate to quote these words—but especially now!

Where now are the glittering trappings of your consulship? Where are the gleaming torches? Where are the rounds of applause, the choral dancing, the banquets, the public festivals? Where are the garlands and the curtains of the theater? Where are the cheers of the city's citizens, the acclamation in the hippodrome, and the flatteries of the theater-goers?

All of that is no more! Suddenly, a wind has blown against the tree, tearing down its leaves, revealing it to be quite bare, and shaken to its very roots. The assault of that

[1]For the original Greek, see PG 52:391B–396C; for an English translation, see NPNF[1] 9:249–52.

wind was so powerful that it shook every fiber of the tree, and threatened to pull it up from the roots.

Where now are the friends gathered around you? Where are the drinking parties, and the feasting? Where is the swarm of parasites, and the wine that used to flow all day long, and the great variety of dishes created by the cooks? And where are those courting your authority, doing and saying everything to gain your favor?

All these things were like a dream in the night, or a fleeting vision in the day. They were like spring flowers, which all withered when spring was over. They were a shadow that has fled away; fruit that has rotted; bubbles that have burst; cobwebs that have been torn apart.

Therefore we continually chant these spiritual words, saying, "Vanity of vanities! All is vanity!" This saying ought to be written continually on our walls, on our garments, in the marketplace, in our homes, along the roadways, on the doors and entrances, and above all on the conscience of each one of us—to be a perpetual subject for meditation. Since the deceitfulness of present things, and masks, and pretense seem to many to be truth, it is needful every day, at dinner and at breakfast, and at community assemblies, to say to one's neighbor, and to hear from one's neighbor, the words: "Vanity of vanities! All is vanity!"

Wealth is a fleeting, untrustworthy servant

Was I not telling you constantly, Eutropius, that wealth is fleeting? But you did not heed us. Was I not telling you that it is an untrustworthy servant? But you did not wish to be persuaded.

But behold now—how your experience of things has shown that not only is wealth fleeting and untrustworthy, but it can also bring about one's demise. For this is what has led to your trembling and fear.

"I love you more"

Did I not say to you when you continually rebuked me for speaking the truth, "But I love you more than those flattering you"? And, "I who reprove you care more for you than those currying your favor"? And did I not add to these words, "The wounds of friends are more trustworthy than the voluntary kisses of enemies"?[2]

If you had heeded my piercing words, their kisses would not have brought about this destruction for you. For my wounding works for health, while their kisses have produced an incurable disease.

Where now are the cupbearers? Where are those who cleared the way for you in the marketplace, who a myriad of times sang your praises to everyone? They have run off; they have disowned their friendship; they are procuring their own safety while leaving you in anguish.

But we do not do that; we do not abandon you in your distress. And now that you have fallen, we protect you and minister to you. And the Church that you made war against has opened her bosom and received you; while the theaters that you frequented—and you often laughed

---

[2] Cf. Prov 27.6.

when I warned you about them—have betrayed you, playing a role in your ruin.

But we never ceased saying to you, "Why are you doing these things? You are vexing the Church, while casting yourself down a precipice." But you spurned all my warnings.

The hippodromes, exhausting your wealth, whetted the sword against you. But the Church, even after enduring your unwarranted wrath, is hurrying in every direction, wishing to pluck you out of the nets.

"Contemplating the vicissitudes of human affairs"

I am saying these things now, not as trampling upon one who is prostrate, but as wishing to make more secure those who are still standing; not as aggravating the sores of one who has been wounded, but as preserving in sound health those who have not yet been wounded; not as pushing downwards one who is being tossed by the waves, but as instructing those who are sailing with fair breezes, so that they might not become submerged. And how might this happen? By contemplating the vicissitudes of human affairs.

Even this man, if he had feared such vicissitudes, would not have endured such a sudden change in fortune. And while neither the counsel of his own conscience nor that of others made him better, may those of you who are proud of your riches profit from his calamity.

Nothing is more fragile than human affairs. Therefore, whatever one says to express their insignificance, it will be short of the truth: whether he calls them smoke, or grass, or a dream, or spring flowers, or any other name. So perishable are they that they partake of nothingness more than nothing itself! Yet together with their nothingness, they have a perilous aspect also, as is evident here before us.

"A soul turned to stone"

For who was more exalted than this man? Did he not surpass the entire world in wealth? Had he not ascended to the very pinnacle of distinction? Did not everyone tremble before him, and fear him?

Yet behold! He has become more wretched than those in bonds, more pitiable than household slaves, more indigent than paupers wasting away with hunger. Every day he has a vision of sharpened swords, a criminal's grave, and the public executioner leading him out to his death. He does not even know whether he once enjoyed past pleasures; he is not even aware of the sun's rays. For his sight is so dimmed that at midday it's as if he were encompassed with the darkest night.

Yet however much we may strive, it's impossible for us to adequately describe his suffering, which he is naturally enduring because of his expectation of being put to death at any hour. But indeed, what need is there of any words from us, when he himself has depicted his agony before us as if in an engraved image? For yesterday, when they came to him from the imperial court, intending to drag him away by force, and he fled to the holy altar here, his face was then, just as it is now, no better than that of one already dead. And the chattering of his teeth, the quaking and quivering of his whole body, his faltering voice, his stammering tongue, and indeed his entire appearance make it look as if his soul has turned to stone.

"To incline you to mercy"

I am saying these things, not to reproach him, or to insult his misfortune, but wishing to soften your disposition towards him, to incline you to mercy, and to persuade you to be content with the punishment that has already come upon him. Since it seems there are many inhumane persons among us who would likewise bring accusation against us for receiving this man into the sanctuary, I desire to soften their heartlessness by shedding light upon the depth of his sufferings.

"The power of the Church and her love for mankind"

Tell me, beloved brother, what are you distressed about? You say it's because he who continually made war against the Church has taken refuge within her. Yet surely we ought to glorify God most especially for permitting him to be subjected to such need, so that he might learn both the power of the Church and her love for mankind—her power, in that he has suffered this great reversal of fortune because of his attacks against her; and her love for mankind, in that she whom he attacked now casts her shield in front of him, receiving him under her wings, and placing him in all security, not resenting anything that he did against her, but rather opening her bosom unto him with great love.[3]

This is more brilliant than any kind of trophy; this is an illustrious victory; this shames the Greeks and disgraces the Jews;[4] this shows the brightness of the Church's face—in that having received her enemy as a captive, she spares him. And when everyone has despised him in his desolation, only she, as a mother filled with tender love, has concealed him under her cloak, over against the wrath of the king, the rage of the people, and their unbearable hatred.

This is an ornament for the altar. A strange kind of ornament, you say?—with one accursed, an extortioner, a robber laying hold of it! No—do not say that. For even the prostitute took hold of the feet of Jesus, she who was accursed and exceedingly unclean. Yet what happened was not a reproach to Jesus; rather, it became the occasion for great wonder and praise for Him. For the impure woman did no injury to the pure one; rather, the vile prostitute was made pure by the touch of the pure and spotless one.

So do not hold a grudge, O man! We are the servants of the Crucified One, who said from the cross, *Forgive them, for they know not what they do* (Lk 23.34).

Eutropius has become a teacher for all

"But," you say, "he cut off his right of refuge here because of his various ordinances and laws against us." But behold! He has learned from what has happened that he should

---

[3]Greek: *pollēs philostorgias.*
[4]I.e., pagans and Jews (see 1 Cor 1).

not have done those things; and through what he has done, he has become the first to break the law, becoming a spectacle to the whole world. And silent though he is, he gives from there a voice of warning to everyone: "Do not do what I have done, so you will not suffer what I am suffering!"

He appears as a teacher through his calamity, and the altar radiates great brilliance, inspiring the greatest awe, now that it holds the lion in bondage. Any king would enjoy great adornment, not just in sitting upon his throne, arrayed in purple and wearing a crown, but also in having barbarians prostrate at his feet, with their hands bound behind their backs, and their heads bending low to the ground.

You yourselves are witnesses that no persuasive arguments were used to bring you here in such great numbers, and with such great zeal. Brilliant indeed is the scene before us today, and magnificent is the multitude assembled, as I see now a gathering such as at holy Pascha! Without speaking a word, this man has summoned you here. Yet, through his actions, he has raised a voice clearer than a trumpet.

And so you have all thronged here today—maidens leaving their rooms empty, matrons the women's quarters, and men the marketplace—to see human nature convicted, and the instability of earthly affairs exposed, and a face like that of a prostitute that only yesterday was radiant but now appears uglier than that of a wrinkled old woman now that its cosmetic paints and pigments have been wiped off by adversity, as if by a sponge (such is prosperity derived from extortion).

Such is the force of this misfortune: it has made one who was illustrious and conspicuous to appear now to be more wretched than all others. And if a wealthy man should enter our assembly here, there is much for him to gain. For when he sees the one who was shaking the whole world now dragged down from such a pinnacle of power, cowering with fright, more terrified than a hare or a frog, fettered to that pillar while yet being untied, encircled by fear instead of a chain, panic-stricken and trembling, then the wealthy man's haughtiness is put in check, his arrogance is brought down, and he gains the wisdom that one in his position needs to have—wisdom that the Scriptures teach in these words: *All flesh is grass; and all the glory of man is like the flower of the grass. The grass withers, and the flower falls* (Is 40.6–7); and, *For they shall soon be withered like the grass, and shall soon fall away as the green herb* (Ps 36.2); and his *days are vanished like smoke* (Ps 102.3); and all such passages.

And the poor man, upon entering here, will also benefit. For upon beholding this spectacle, he does not belittle himself, neither does he bewail his poverty. Rather, he becomes grateful for his penury, realizing it is a place of safety for him, a calm harbor, a secure bulwark. Seeing these things, he would much rather remain as he is than possess everything for a little while and then be in danger of losing his life.

Do you see how there has been no little gain for the rich and the poor, the high and the low, slaves and free men, on account of this man fleeing here for refuge? Do you see how each one will leave here with a remedy, having been cured simply by this sight?

"Have I led you to compassion?"

So! Have I quelled your passion? Have I expelled your wrath? Have I extinguished your inhumanity? Have I led you to compassion? I very much believe I have. Your faces make this evident, especially the streams of your tears. Since your stony heart has now become deep and fertile ground, let us hasten to blossom forth with some fruit of mercy, and to display a luxuriant crop of sympathy, by falling down before the emperor—or rather, by beseeching our God who loves mankind to melt away the wrath of the emperor, to make his heart tender, so that he would grant to all of us the favor we are asking for.

The tears of the emperor

And actually, already, since that day when this man fled here for refuge, no little change has taken place. For as soon as the emperor knew that the man had run to this place of sanctuary, and although the army was present, incensed on account of the man's misdeeds and demanding that he be turned over for execution, he made a long speech to allay the wrath of the soldiers, urging that not only the man's sinful acts, but also any good deeds he may have done, be taken into account. The emperor declared that he felt gratitude for the good things the man did, and that he was ready to pardon him, as a fellow human being, for what he had done wrong.

When the soldiers, with shouting and leaping, and brandishing their spears in their thirst for blood, again urged him to avenge the man's outrageous acts done against the imperial majesty, streams of tears flowed from the emperor's gentle eyes. And reminding them of the holy table to which the man fled, he succeeded in bringing their wrath to an end.

Now is the time for mercy

Let me now add a few things that concern us all. What pardon could you deserve, if when the emperor, gravely insulted as he was, bears no malice, you, who have endured nothing of that kind, display so much animosity? And how, after this spectacle is over, will you handle the holy Mysteries, and how will you repeat that prayer that we are commanded to say, "Forgive us, as we forgive our debtors," when you are demanding vengeance against the one offending you?

Has he inflicted great wrongs and insults upon you? I do not deny it. But now is not the time for judgment, but for mercy; not for requiring an account, but for loving-kindness;[5] not for scrutiny, but for concession; not for verdicts and vengeance, but for compassion and favor.

Let no one, then, be irritated or vexed. Let us rather beseech the God who loves mankind to grant him a

---

[5]Greek: *philanthrōpias.*

continuation of life, to rescue him from the impending destruction, so that he may put aside his transgressions. And let us approach in unison the benevolent[6] emperor for the sake of the Church, for the sake of the altar, so that one man might be granted favor out of regard for the holy table.

If we do this, the emperor himself will accept us; and even beyond the praise of the emperor, God will grant us a great recompense for our love for mankind. For as He rejects and hates one who is cruel and inhuman, so He welcomes and loves one who is merciful, one who loves mankind. And if such a one is righteous, He will weave a crown for him that is all the more brilliant. And if he is a sinner, He passes over his sins as a reward for showing compassion to his fellow-servant. *For I desire mercy*, He says, *and not sacrifice* (Hosea 6.6). And throughout the Scriptures, you will see Him always seeking after this, and declaring it to be the means for the release from sins.

Thus, then, we shall render Him propitious towards us; thus we shall release ourselves from our sins; thus we shall adorn the Church; thus our benevolent emperor, as I have said, will commend us; and all the people will applaud us; and the ends of the earth will marvel at the love for mankind, and the tender gentleness, of our city; and all those everywhere who learn of these things will proclaim and extol us.

That we may enjoy these good things, let us fall to our knees, let us implore, let us beseech, let us supplicate. Let

[6]Greek: *philanthrōpō*

us rescue the captive, the fugitive, the supplicant, from the danger, so that we ourselves may obtain the future good things, through the grace and love for mankind of our Lord Jesus Christ, to whom be glory and power, now and ever, and unto ages of ages. Amen.

Homily on Those Seeking Sanctuary

A note on the text

Although this homily is usually designated as St John Chrysostom's *Homily II on Eutropius* (or "On the Capture of Eutropius"), it is very clear from internal evidence that he did not preach it about Eutropius, who received clemency after taking refuge in the Hagia Sophia Cathedral in the capital city, after the great preacher had calmed the rage and vindictiveness of the people, as we saw in the previous sermon. St John had also referred in that sermon to the merciful tears of Emperor Arcadius, which he shed for Eutropius. So the eunuch had no reason to flee from the church.

There are no indications in this sermon of the one seeking refuge finding mercy from the emperor, which is perhaps why he felt he had to abandon the church, at which point he was captured—although he was later released. This person most likely was Count John, a highly placed imperial courtier and close friend of Empress Eudoxia, who had been sought as a hostage by the Gothic general, Gainus. This Gainus was a general serving the empire, but he was intent upon increasing his influence and power within it, and it was most probable that his soldiers would prove to be more loyal to him than to the emperor if their general commanded them to storm the imperial palace.

So this explains how it is that as Count John (assuming he is the one) was huddled in the Hagia Sophia Cathedral seeking protection, Gainus' Gothic/Germanic soldiers were enraged and threatening, "with swords unsheathed," outside the cathedral; as Chrysostom says in his sermon, "the fury of the soldiers was fiercer than fire." And when he then says that "I was whisked away to the imperial palace," this was done by imperial guards in order for him to play a diplomatic role in the effort to calm Gainus, so that his unruly troops would no longer be a threat to the peace and order of the city. And it was the threat of those troops while he was being taken by the imperial guards to the palace that caused St John to say in this sermon, as he was recounting these events, "I saw the swords, and thought about Heaven. I expected to die, and thought about the resurrection."[1]

St John's vivid, dramatic account of the recent tumultuous events that involved him and Count John, including

---

[1]For more on this particular understanding of the context for this sermon, see Kelly, *Golden Mouth,* 151–56.

his inspiring descriptions of his response to these events, reveal his fearlessness in the face of any kind of tribulation in this life and indicate much about his deep emotional stability and spiritual maturity in the face of danger and hardship. Perhaps they also foreshadow the personal descriptions of his sufferings and his response to them that he shared in seventeen letters written to his intimate confidante, the deaconess St Olympia, several years later, while he was in exile.[2]

As in the previous homily, St John again talks about the transience of wealth—"Do you really wish to court it? Do you wish to hold it fast? Then do not bury it, but give it into the hands of the poor"; and of power—"Have you seen the paltriness of human affairs? Have you beheld the fragility of political power?" But his main emphasis proves to be the Lord's ineffably all-forgiving and all-embracing love for humanity, for human nature, for "the harlot" whom He desires and pursues to make her His own, and to make her pure and holy, through becoming one with her in taking her humanity through His incarnation. This is probably the most moving account in all of Chrysostom's vast writings of our Lord's infinite love, which moves Him to become incarnate for us.

In this remarkable and lengthy homily, St John also speaks powerfully of the twofold dowry that Christ gives His Bride—manifold blessings bestowed in this life

---

[2]See St John Chrysostom, *Letters to Saint Olympia*, trans. David C. Ford, Popular Patristics Series 56 (Yonkers, NY: St Vladimir's Seminary Press, 2016).

(which together comprise "the earnest of the Spirit"), and many more that are reserved for the next life. As St John has Christ tell her, "You have the Master as your Lover. And since you have Him as your Lover, you also have the things of His."

St John also presents, in this often-overlooked sermon, a wonderful description of the glory and strength of the Church, a dramatic discussion of the use of human terminology in the Scriptures to describe truths about God and his activities, and an insightful consideration of physical and noetic beauty. Besides all this, he begins this homily with a very brief but typically eloquent rhapsody on another favorite theme of his—the great benefits of reading the Holy Scriptures.

Homily on Another Fugitive Seeking Sanctuary in the Cathedral of Hagia Sophia[3]

The sweetness and power of the Scriptures

Sweet are the meadow and the garden, but sweeter by far is the reading of the divine Scriptures. For there, the flowers fade; while here, spiritual thoughts abide in full bloom. There, breezes of the wind; here, the breath of the Spirit. There, hedges of thorns; here, the protecting Providence of God. There, the singing of the cicadas; here, the melody of the prophets. There, delights that are seen; here, benefits that come from reading. A garden exists in one place, while the Scriptures abound throughout the world. A garden is subject to the exigencies of the seasons, while the

[3]PG 52:395D–414C; NPNF¹ 9:252–65.

Scriptures flourish in foliage and are laden with fruit in winter as well as in summer.

So let us give attention to the study of the Scriptures. For if you do this, the Scriptures will drive out your despondency; they will bring forth pleasure,[4] uproot vice, and implant virtue; and in the tumult of life they will not let you flounder as those who are tossed about by the waves. The sea rages, but you travel along as in a great calm, for you have the study of the Scriptures as your pilot. This is the rope that the trials of life do not tear apart.

Recent events

That I am not lying, recent events bear witness. For a few days ago the Church was besieged. An army came; fire was in their eyes, yet it did not scorch the olive tree. Swords were unsheathed, yet no one received a wound. The gates of the imperial palace were embattled, but the Church was in security.

Yet the tide of war turned here as well, for the fugitive sought refuge here. Yet we withstood them, not fearing their fury. And why was this? Because we had the steadfast pledge, *Thou art Peter, and on this rock I will build My Church, and the gates of hell will not prevail against her* (Mt 16.18). And when I say "the Church," I do not only refer to a place [*topon*], but also to a way of life [*tropon*]—not to the walls of the Church, but to her laws. For when you take refuge in the Church, you do not seek shelter primarily in

---

[4]Greek: *hēdonēn*.

a place, but in her wisdom and judgment. For the Church is not primarily wall and roof, but faith and life.

Do not say that the one who was captured was handed over by the Church. If he had not abandoned the Church, he would not have been captured.

Do not say that he fled here and was betrayed by the Church. For the Church did not abandon him; rather, he abandoned the Church. He was not turned over from inside the Church; rather, he went outside the Church, and was apprehended there.

Why did he forsake the Church? O fugitive, did you wish to be saved? You should have held fast to the altar! You would have been protected not so much by the Church's walls, as by the Providence of God. Were you a sinful man? God would not have rejected you for that, for He *did not come to call the righteous, but sinners, to repentance* (Mk 2.17; Lk 5.32). The prostitute was saved when she clung to His feet. Did you not hear about that in today's reading in the Church?[5]

I say these things so that none of you would ever be hesitant to flee to the Church. Remain within the Church, and she will never abandon you to those outside, for she is not like the world. But if you leave the Church, then she is not responsible for your capture. If you remain within, the wolf will not enter to seize you. But if you leave, you become its prey. This is not the fault of the sheepfold; rather, it is because of your own lack of faith.

[5]Lk 7.36–50.

Do not tell me about walls and weapons; for walls grow old with time, but the Church never grows old. Barbarians can batter down walls, but the Church is not overcome even by demons.

That my words are not mere boasting, events bear witness. How many have waged war against her through the years?—and yet they have perished, while the Church has soared above the heavens! Such might the Church has: when she is assailed, she conquers; when she is plotted against, she overcomes; when she is despitefully treated, she shines all the more brightly; when she receives wounds, she is not brought low by them; when she is tossed by the waves, she is not submerged; when she is assaulted by storms, she suffers no shipwreck; she wrestles, yet is not weakened; she fights, but is not vanquished.

So why did the Church meet with this recent war? So that her victory would shine forth all the more brightly. You were present that day; you saw what weapons were raised against her, and how the fury of the soldiers was fiercer than fire, and how I was whisked away to the imperial palace. But what of that? By the grace of God, none of these things dismayed me.

I am saying these things so that you might mimic me. Why was I not dismayed? Because I do not fear any of the terrors that can happen in this life. What are those terrors? Death? It is not a terror, for by it we are speedily ushered into the undisturbed harbor of Heaven. The confiscation of one's property? *Naked I came from my mother's womb, and naked will I depart* (Job 1.21). Exile? *The earth is the Lord's, and the fullness thereof* (Ps 23.1). Defamation? *Rejoice and exult when they say all manner of evil against you falsely; for great is your reward in Heaven* (Mt 5.11–12).

I saw the swords, and thought about Heaven. I expected to die, and thought about the resurrection. I beheld the sufferings here below, and numbered the prizes above. I saw the plots, and considered the heavenly crowns. The occasion of the contest was sufficient for consolation and encouragement.

True, I was led away against my will, but that was not an outrage against me. There is only one real outrage, and that is sin. Even if the entire world treats you despitefully, if you do not bring disgrace upon yourself, you will not be disgraced. The only tribunal that can really bring you to punishment is your own conscience. If you do not bring the condemnation of your conscience upon yourself, then no one can condemn you.

I was being led away, beholding what was transpiring— or rather, my own words were becoming reality, the words I had previously preached. For the words of that homily of mine were taking shape in the marketplace; they were being preached again through what was happening. And what was that homily about? What I always preach on: the wind blows, and the leaves fall. *The grass has withered up, and the flower has faded* (Is 40.7).

Night has departed; the day has appeared. The shadow has been confuted; the truth has appeared.

They ascended up to the heavens and descended to the surface of the earth; the waves, once so high, have been brought low through human events. How so? The events themselves did the teaching; the lessons were ringing in our ears.

Yet I asked myself, "Will posterity learn to be prudent from these things? Or will this lesson be given over to oblivion after two days?"

Let me speak again; I will speak once more. To what profit? Yet there will be profit. For even if not all the people hearken, half of them will. And if not half, a third. And if not a third, a fourth. And if not a fourth, there may be ten. And if not ten, there may be five. And if not five, there may be one. And if not one, I myself will receive the reward prepared for me. *The grass has withered up, the flower has faded; but the word of God remains forever* (Is 40.7–8).

The impotence of wealth

Have you seen the paltriness of human affairs? Have you beheld the fragility of political power? Have you seen the wealth that I have always called a runaway—and not only a runaway, but a murderer also? For it not only deserts those having it, but it also slays them. For if anyone pays court to it, then especially does it betray him. Why do you pay court to wealth that today is yours but tomorrow belongs to someone else? Why do you court wealth, which is never possible to hold fast?

Do you really wish to court it? Do you wish to hold it fast? Then do not bury it, but give it into the hands of the poor.

Wealth is like a wild animal: if you try to hold it tightly, it runs away; but if it is let loose, it stays put. For, it is said, *he has dispersed his wealth; he has given to the poor; his righteousness endures forevermore* (Ps 111.9; 2 Cor 9.9). So disperse it, so that it will remain; do not bury it, so that it does not flee away.

"Where is your wealth?"—I would gladly ask the departed. But I say these things, not in reproach—God forbid!—and not to aggravate old wounds, but in order to prepare a harbor for you from the shipwrecks of others.

When the soldiers came with swords unsheathed; when the city was aflame with fury; when the imperial authority was powerless; when the imperial purple was affronted; when frenzy was everywhere, where was your wealth, O fugitive? Where were your wares of silver? Where were your silver couches? Where were your household servants? They all had fled. Where were the eunuchs? They had all run away. Where were your friends? They had changed their masks. Where were your homes? They were bolted shut. Where was your money? Those keeping it fled away. And where was the money left? It was buried. And where was it hidden?

Am I burdensome to you all, am I being oppressive, as I am forever saying that wealth betrays those who use it badly? Now the time[6] has come that proves the truthfulness of my words. Why do you cling tightly to your wealth, when in a time of trial it's of no benefit? If it does have power to help you when you fall into a desperate plight,

---

[6]Greek: *kairos.*

then let it stand by you. But if instead it flees away, what need do you have for it?

Recent events have borne witness to this. What benefit was your wealth when the sword was whetted, death was threatening, the army was enraged, catastrophe was imminent? It was nowhere to be found! Where had that runaway fled? It was the cause itself of all these things, yet in your time of need it flees away!

Yet many reproach me, saying, "You're always harping against the rich!"—while they themselves forever inveigh against the poor. I do harp against the rich—yet not the rich, but those who make bad use of their wealth. For I'm continually saying that I do not attack the wealthy, but the rapacious. A rich person is one thing; one who is rapacious is another. Someone who is affluent is one thing; someone who is covetous is another. Make clear distinctions; do not mix together diverse things.

Are you rich? I do not forbid you. Are you rapacious? Then I denounce you! Do you have things of your own? Enjoy them. But did you take the goods of others? I will not keep silent! Do you wish to stone me for this? I am ready to shed my blood. Only I will forbid your sin. I am not concerned about hatred against me; I am not concerned about war against me. One thing only am I concerned about, and that is the spiritual progress of my hearers.

The rich are my children; the poor also are my children. The same womb travailed to give birth to them both; they were both brought forth with the same birth pangs.

If you reproach one who is poor, I will accuse you, since the poor have fewer goods to be responsible for than the rich have. The penalty for not being generous that you rich will suffer is much greater than that endured by the poor man if he is not generous, since he has much less money to be generous with.[7] Cut me off, if you wish, for saying this; stone me if you wish; hate me if you wish. For plots against me are the pledge of heavenly crowns for me, which will be as many as the number of my wounds.

St John's fearlessness

I am not afraid of plots. There is only one thing I fear, and that is sin. As long as no one accuses me of sinning, let the whole world wage war against me! War like that makes me more lustrous.

I wish to instruct you further. Do not fear the plots of rulers against you; rather, fear the power of sin. Men cannot injure you if you do not strike yourself. If you are free from sin, if a myriad of drawn swords appear against you, God will seize you and snatch you away from them. But if you are abiding in sin, even if you are in Paradise, you will be cast out.

Adam was in Paradise, yet he fell. Job sat upon a dunghill and was crowned. What benefit for Adam was Paradise? What harm to Job was the dunghill? No one plotted against Adam, yet he was overthrown. The devil plotted against Job, and he was crowned. "Didn't the devil seize his property?" you say. Yes, but he did not rob him of his

---

[7] The Greek of this sentence is obscure.

godliness. "Didn't he seize his children?" Yes, but he did not shake his faith. "Didn't he tear Job's body?" Yes, but he did not touch his heart. "Didn't he arm his wife against him?" Yes, but he did not overthrow the soldier. "Didn't he hurl arrows and darts at him?" Yes, but he received no wounds. The devil brought on his engines of war but did not shake the tower. He stirred up waves but did not sink the ship.

I beseech you, keep this law for me; I clasp your knees— if not literally, yet in spirit; I pour forth tears. Observe this law, and no one will be able to injure you. Never call the rich man blessed; never call anyone miserable except the one abiding in sin; and consider blessed the one living in righteousness. For it is not the nature of their circumstances, but the disposition of their hearts, that makes both kinds of people.

Never be afraid of the sword if your conscience does not accuse you; never fear war, if your conscience is clean.

Where now, tell me, have they gone?—those who but yesterday everyone bowed down to. Didn't even men in authority tremble at them? Did they not pay court to them? But sin has come, and everything has been revealed. Those who were his attendants have become his judges; those who flattered him have become his executioners. Those who kissed his hands are the very ones who dragged him away from the church. He who yesterday kissed his hands is today his enemy. How is this? Because he did not love him before with sincerity.

For the time[8] came, and the masks came off. Didn't you kiss his hands yesterday, and regard him as a savior, a guardian, a benefactor? Didn't you weave for him a myriad of accolades? So why do you accuse him today? Why yesterday praising, and today accusing? Why yesterday *encomia*, and today condemnations? Why this change? Why this revolution?

But I was not like that. I was the subject of his plots, but I became his protector. I suffered a myriad of fearsome things, but I did not retaliate. For I imitate my own Master, who said from the cross, *Forgive them, for they know not what they do* (Lk 23.34).

St John's pastoral heart

I say these things lest you be deceived by suspicions spread by evil men. How many changes have taken place since I was placed in authority over this city, and is there no one who is prudent? Yet I do not condemn everyone—God forbid! For it is not the case that this fertile soil, having received good seed, has not brought forth a single ear of corn!

Yet I am insatiable! For I do not want just a few to be saved, but everyone! If but one is left perishing, I perish as well. I consider that the shepherd should be imitated who had ninety-nine sheep, yet hastened after the one that had gone astray.

[8]Greek: *kairos.*

The transience of this life

How long will money last? How long silver? How long gold? How long the enjoyment of wine? How long the flatteries of servants? How long garlanded goblets? How long satanic feasts, filled with diabolical activity?

Don't you know that this present life is a sojourn away from home? Are you a citizen? No, you are a wayfarer. Are you comprehending what I am saying? You are not a citizen, but a wayfarer, a sojourner. Do not tell me, "I have this or that city." No one has a city here below. The city is above. The present life is but a road. We are journeying onwards day by day, while nature runs its course.

Some there are who put aside possessions along the way; some bury gold along the road. But tell me, when you reach the inn, do you beautify it? Certainly not! You just eat and drink and then hasten to depart.

The present life is an inn; we have entered it, and here we spend the present life. Let us be diligent to leave it with a good hope. Let us leave nothing here, so that we may not lose it there.

Whenever you enter an inn, what do you say to the servant? "Take care where you put our things, so that nothing will be left behind here, so that nothing will be lost, no matter how small, no matter how trifling, so that we may carry everything back to our home."

You are a wayfarer, a traveler; indeed, you are more insignificant than a traveler. How so? I will tell you. The traveler knows when he will enter the inn, and when he will leave; he is in charge of his comings and goings. But when I enter this inn—that is, the present life—I do not know when I will leave it. It may be that I'm storing up provisions for myself for a long time to come, and the Lord suddenly calls me, saying, "You fool! Who will get those things you've been storing up for yourself? This night they are taking your soul."[9]

Yes—the time of your departure is uncertain, your goods are insecure; for there are a myriad of precipices, and waves are everywhere. So why do you boast madly about shadows? Why do you forsake reality and run after shadows?

I say these things, and I will not stop saying these things, continually causing pain yet dressing the wounds, not for the sake of those who have fallen away, but for those still standing. For those who have departed have met their end, while those still standing have been made more secure by the calamities they have gone through.

"What then," you say, "shall we do?" Do one thing only: hate riches, and love your life.[10] Cast away your possessions—I don't mean everything, but cut off what you have that is superfluous. Don't desire what belongs to others; don't plunder the widows and the orphans—don't seize their homes. I'm not accusing anyone; I'm merely stating facts. If anyone's conscience afflicts him, it's because of his own deeds, not my words.

Why do you grasp [for worldly things], bringing malice against yourself? Grasp for a crown! Grasp not the

[9]See Lk 12.16–21.
[10]Greek: *zōēn*.

earth, but Heaven! "For the Kingdom of Heaven belongs to those who are violent; those who are violent seize it."[11]

Why do you lay hold of a poor person if he accuses you of something? Lay hold of Christ, that He may praise you! Do you see your senselessness and madness? Do you lay hold of the poor one who has little? Christ says, "Seize Me, seize My Kingdom and take it by force, and I will be well-pleased."

If you devise a plot to seize an earthly kingdom, you are punished; if you do not seize the heavenly Kingdom, you will be punished. Where earthly things are concerned, there is envy; but where spiritual things are concerned, there is love.[12]

Meditate on these things every day, and if in two days you behold someone being carried along in a chariot, arrayed in silken garments, and elated with pride, don't be troubled or shaken. Don't praise the rich; only praise those living in righteousness. Don't revile the poor; but rather, learn to have precise, unerring judgment in all things.

The strength and glory of the Church

Don't hold yourself apart from the Church; for nothing is stronger than the Church. The Church is your hope; the Church is your salvation; the Church is your refuge. She is higher than the heavens, and wider than the earth. She never grows old; she is forever full of vigor. Because of her

---

[11] See Mt 11.12.
[12] Greek: *agapē*.

solidity and stability, the Scripture calls her a *mountain*;[13] because of her purity, it calls her a *virgin*;[14] because of her magnificence, it calls her *Queen* (Ps 44.10); regarding her relationship with God, it calls her *daughter*;[15] regarding how prolific she is, it calls her *the barren one who has given birth to seven* (1 Sam 2.5).

The Scripture indeed employs a myriad of names to indicate her nobility. Just as her Master is called many names—*Father*, and the *Way*, and the *Life*, and the *Light*, and the *Arm*, and the *Propitiation*, and the *Foundation*, and the *Door*, and the *sinless One*, and the *Treasure,* and the *Lord*, and *God*, and *Only-Begotten*, and the *form of God*, and the *image of God*—so also it is with the Church.[16]

Is one name sufficient to designate the whole truth? By no means! Rather, a multitude of names are used, so that we may learn something about God, even if it's just a little. So also the Church is called by many names. She is called a virgin, even though formerly she was a harlot.[17] Indeed, this is the Bridegroom's miracle—that He took a harlot and made her a virgin. O what a new and paradoxical event! With us, marriage dissolves virginity; but with God,

[13]See Is. 2.2–3; Mic 4.1–2.

[14]See 2 Cor 11.2.

[15]See Ps 44.11–14.

[16]*Father* (Is 9.6); *Way* (Jn 14.6); *Life* (Jn 14.6); *Light* (Jn 8.12); *Arm* (Is 53.1–2); *Propitiation* (1 Jn 2.2); *Foundation* (see Ps 117.22); *Door* (Jn 10.7 and 9); *sinless One* (Heb 4.15); *Treasure* (see Mt 13.44); *Lord* (1 Cor 12.3); *God* (Rom 9.5); *Only-Begotten* (Jn 3.16); *form of God* (Phil 2.6); *image of God* (Heb 1.3).

[17]See Hos 2.2–20.

marriage has restored virginity. With us, the one who is a virgin, upon getting married, is a virgin no longer; but with God, the one who is a harlot, upon marrying [Him], becomes a virgin.

Let the heretic—the one who busies himself with curiosity about the heavenly generation [of the Son], saying, "How did the Father generate the Son?"—explain this one fact: How did the Church, having been a harlot, become a virgin? And how has she remained a virgin while bringing forth many children? For Paul says, *I am jealous over you with a godly jealousy, for I have espoused you to one husband, that I might present you a pure virgin to Christ* (2 Cor 11.2). O what wisdom and understanding!

Human terminology for God and His actions

I am jealous over you with a godly jealousy. What does this mean when he says, "I am jealous"? Are you really jealous, Paul, being a spiritual man? "I am jealous," he says, "as God is jealous." And is God jealous? Yes, He is jealous—not out of passion, but out of love,[18] and earnest zeal.

"For I am jealous over you with the jealousy of God." Shall I tell you how God is jealous? He saw the world being corrupted by demons, and He delivered over His Son to save it.

Moreover, words spoken in reference to God do not have the same force as when spoken in reference to ourselves. For example, when we say: "God is jealous," "God is angry," "God repents," "God hates"—such words are

---

[18]Greek: *agapē.*

human, but they can convey a meaning that is appropriate to God.

Does God become jealous? "I am jealous over you with the jealousy of God." Does God become angry? *O Lord, rebuke me not in Thine anger* (Ps 6.2). Does God sleep? *Awake! Why sleepest Thou, O Lord?* (Ps 43.23). Does God repent? *I repent that I have made man* (Gen 6.7). Does God hate? *My soul hates your feasts and your new moons* (Is 1.14). But do not cling to these expressions, taking them in a human way. Rather, take their meaning in a way that is appropriate to God.

God is jealous because He loves.[19] God is angry, not out of passion, but in reference to our chastisement and punishment. God sleeps, not as actually slumbering, but as being long-suffering. Be discerning about the expressions. God uses many such words taken from us. And we use some words given to us by God. So when you hear that God "generates" the Son, do not think of a separation, but of the sameness of essence [*homoousion*]. In both cases, we are honored thereby.

Have you understood what I have said? Pay attention with precision, beloved. For there are divine names, and there are human names. God has received some from us, and some He has given to us. "Give Me yours, and receive Mine," He says. "You have need of Mine; I do not have need of yours, but you need Mine. Surely My nature is unmixed, while you are a human being, encompassed with a body, seeking therefore corporeal expressions, so

[19]Greek: *agapa*.

that you, being encompassed with a body, by using words that are familiar to you, may contemplate [*noēsēs*] things [*noēmata*][20] that transcend you."

What sort of names has He taken from me, and what sort has He given me? He Himself is God, and He has called me "god"; but He is God by nature, while I am called "god" by honor: *I have said, "Ye are gods, and all of you are sons of the Most High"* (Ps 81.6; Jn 10.34). Referring to us, it's just an expression; but referring to God, it's the actual reality.

He has called me "god," thereby honoring me, while He was called "man," and *Son of Man*,[21] and the *Way*, and the *Door*, and the *Rock*.[22] These names He has taken from me; the other word He Himself gave to me.

Why was He called the "Way"? So that you might learn that we are guided to the Father by Him. Why was He called the "Rock"? That you might learn the usefulness and unshakeableness of faith. Why was He called the "Foundation"? That you might learn that He supports all things. And why the "Root"?[23] For you to learn that we are to blossom in Him. And why "Shepherd"?[24] Because He

---

[20]These two Greek words come from the word *nous*, which can be translated as "mind" or "intellect"; but in time, in the Christian spiritual tradition, *nous* comes to refer to the deepest place in the heart, the faculty by which knowledge about divine things is perceived.

[21]E.g., Mt 18.11.

[22]1 Cor 10.4.

[23]See Rev 5.5.

[24]Jn 10.11 and 14.

tends us. And why a "Sheep"?[25] Because He was sacrificed for us, through becoming a propitiatory offering. And why "Life"?[26] Because He raised us up when we were dead. And why "Light"? Because He delivered us from darkness. And why "Arm"? Because He is of one essence [*homoousios*] with the Father.[27] And why "Word"?[28] Because He was begotten of the Father; for just as my speech is generated from within my soul, so the Son was generated from the Father.

And why is He called "Raiment"? Because I was clothed with Him when I was baptized.[29] And why a "Table"? Because I feed upon Him when I enjoy the Mysteries. And why a "House"? Because I dwell in Him. And why is He called a Dweller in the house? Because we become His temple.[30] And why "Head"?[31] Because I have been made a member of His. And why the "Bridegroom"?[32] Because He took me as a virgin. And why "Master"? Because I am His bondmaid.[33]

Behold, the Church, as I was saying, is sometimes called "Bride," sometimes "Daughter," sometimes "Virgin,"

---

[25]See Jn 1.29 and 36.

[26]E.g., Jn 14.6.

[27]This is the most crucial Christological term in the Nicene Creed, composed at the First Ecumenical Council, held in Nicaea in 325.

[28]Greek: *Logos* (Jn 1.1).

[29]See Gal 3.27.

[30]See 1 Cor 6.19.

[31]See Col 1.18 and 2.19; Eph 1.22, 4.15, and 5.23.

[32]Mk 2.19; Jn 3.29.

[33]Greek: *doulē*.

sometimes "Handmaiden," sometimes "Queen," sometimes "a barren woman,"[34] sometimes a "mountain," sometimes "paradise," sometimes "fruitful with children," sometimes a "lily," sometimes a "fountain." For she is all these things.

Yet having heard these expressions, do not take them in a physical sense, I beseech you. Stretch your thinking further. It is not possible that these names could be indicating corporeal realities. For example, a mountain is not a virginal maiden, and an unbetrothed maiden is not the Bride, and the Queen is not a handmaiden; yet the Church is all of these. How can this be? Because these things are not corporeal, but spiritual. In the material realm, these things are narrowly confined and understood. But in the spiritual realm, these same words have a much wider range of meaning.

At Thy right hand stood the Queen (Ps 44.10). The "Queen"? She who was downtrodden and poor—how did she become a Queen? And where did she ascend? She stood high by the side of the King. How? Because the King became a servant. He was not that by nature, but He became so.

Understand, therefore, the things of the Godhead, and be wise about the divine economy.[35] Understand what He was, and what He became for your sake. Do not mix together distinct realities, and do not make what came

[34]See Is 54.1.
[35]Greek: *oikonomias.*

from His love for mankind an occasion for blasphemy.[36] He was lofty, and she [for whom He came] was lowly. He was lofty, not in position, but in nature. He was unmixed, His essence indestructible. His [divine] nature was incorruptible, beyond intelligibility, invisible, beyond comprehension, eternal, unchanging, transcending the nature of angels, higher than the powers above, overpowering human reasoning, surpassing human thought, impossible to be apprehended by sight—only by faith. Angels beheld Him, and trembled; the cherubim veiled themselves with their wings, completely in awe of Him.

He looked upon the earth, and made it tremble (see Is 14.16; Hab 3.6); He threatened the sea, and dried it up (see Is 51.10). He brought rivers out of the desert; He *weighed the mountains in scales, and the valleys in a balance* (Is 40.12).

In what way shall I speak? How will I present the truth? His greatness has no boundaries; His wisdom is beyond calculation; His judgments are untraceable; His ways are unsearchable. Such is His greatness, if it's safe to speak like this, as He is so great.

But what am I to do? I am but a man, and I reason and talk as a man; my tongue is made of clay; I beg forgiveness from the Lord. I use these words not because I have lost my senses, but because of my poverty, and because of the weakness of the nature of my tongue, human as it is.

---

[36]St John is referring to those who would take the incarnation to mean that because Christ became fully human out of His love for mankind, He could not also have been fully God.

Have mercy on me, Master! I do not use these words out of senselessness, but because I have no others. Yet I do not stay fixed upon these paltry words, for I mount up on the wings of understanding that is beyond all words.

Such is His greatness. I say these things so that, without dwelling upon the words, or on the poverty of the expressions, you may learn to do likewise. Why do you marvel if I do this?—for He does the same thing when He wishes to present something to us that transcends human powers of comprehension. Since He is addressing human beings, He uses human imagery,[37] which is indeed sufficient to represent what is being spoken of. While it cannot lead one to the full measure of comprehension, it is adequate in light of the limited powers of the hearers.

Stretch yourselves! Don't grow weary from the prolonged nature of my oration. Just as God, when He manifests Himself, does not do so as He really is, neither does He manifest His bare essence (for no one has seen God as He really is. For even when He condescended to manifest Himself partially, the cherubim trembled; He condescended, and the mountains smoked; He condescended, and the heavens were shaken. For if He did not condescend to only manifest Himself partially, who could bear it?)—as then, I say, He does not manifest Himself as He truly is, but only as the beholder is able to behold Him, so does He appear sometimes as an old man,[38] sometimes as a youth, sometimes in fire,[39] sometimes in a morning breeze, sometimes

[37] *Eikosin*—the Greek word for "icon."
[38] Cf. Dan 7.9.
[39] Cf. Ex 3.6.

in water, sometimes in weapons—all without changing His essential nature, but fashioning His appearance according to the condition of those beholding Him.

On Christ's Transfiguration on Mount Tabor

Accordingly, when one wishes to say something about Him, one uses human imagery. For example, it is said that He went up into a mountain *and was transfigured before them, and His face shone as the sun, and His garments became as white as snow* (Mt 17.1–2). With this, we can say, He disclosed a little of His Godhead, as He showed forth God dwelling among them.

And He was transfigured before them. Pay close attention to what is being said. He says, *And He was transfigured before them, and His garments shone as the light, and His visage as the sun*. When I said, "Such is His greatness," and, "Be merciful to me, Master!" (for I do not remain content with my words; but I am perplexed, having no others to serve my purpose), I desire you to learn that I was instructed in this way by the Scriptures. For the Evangelist, wishing to express His brightness, says, "He shone." How did He shine? Tell me. "Exceedingly." And how do you express this? "As the sun." "As the sun," you say? "Yes." And why do you say this? "Because I know of no other star more brilliant." *And He was white as snow* (v. 2). Why do you say, "as snow"? "Because I know of no other substance that is whiter."

That He did not really shine like that is indicated by what follows. For the disciples fell to the ground. If He had shone as the sun, the disciples would not have fallen.

For they were used to seeing the sun day by day, and had never fallen down thereby. But since He really shone *more brightly* than the sun, and *more brilliantly* than the snow, this is why they could not bear the brightness, and so they fell down.

Explain to me, therefore, O Evangelist, how it is that He shone *more brightly* than the sun, and yet you say, "*as* the sun"? "Yes," he says, "because in wishing to make known to you that light, with no other star being more brilliant, I had no other image among the stars that has a higher place to use as an image."

I've said these things so that you do not rest content with the commonness of the words being used. I have shown you the disciples' fall; for they fell to the earth, stupefied and overcome with sleep. "Arise," He said to them, and He lifted them up; yet still they were weighed down. For they could not endure the magnitude of the brightness, and heavy sleep took possession of their eyes—by so much was that light brighter than the sun. Yet the Evangelist said "as the sun" for this star is familiar to us, exceeding all the other stars in brightness.

God desired a harlot

But as I was saying, this One of such greatness ardently desired a harlot.[40] God desired a harlot? Yes, a harlot, for I speak of our human nature in this way. God desired a harlot? If a man desires a harlot, he is condemned. Yet God desired a harlot? Yes, entirely so! Again, when a man

---

[40] Greek: *epethymēse pornēs.*

desires a harlot, he becomes a fornicator. But when God desires a harlot, He makes her a virgin. The desire of the man works the destruction of the one desired; but the desire of God works the salvation of her who is desired.

One so great desired a harlot? Yes. And why? In order to become her Bridegroom. How does He do this? He does not send to her any of His servants; He does not send an angel to her, or an archangel, or the cherubim, or the seraphim. Rather, He Himself, the one ardently loving[41] her, draws near.

When you hear of ardent love,[42] don't think of anything sensual. Draw out the deeper meaning from the words, just as the excellent bee that settles upon the flowers takes the pollen and leaves the plants.

He desired a harlot, and what does He do? He does not lead her up on high, for He did not wish to lead a harlot into Heaven. Rather, He Himself comes down. Since it was impossible for her to ascend on high, He Himself came down. He comes to the harlot, and is not ashamed. He comes to her in her lowly dwelling. He beholds her in her drunkenness.

And how does He come? Not in a naked manifestation of His essence,[43] but He becomes that which the harlot was. Not in intention only, but in full reality, He takes her nature,[44] so that beholding Him she would not be fright-

---

[41]Greek: *ho erōn.*
[42]Greek: *erōta.*
[43]Greek: *ousia.*
[44]Greek: *physei.*

ened, so that she would not rush away, so that she would not escape.

In order to come to the harlot, He becomes man. And how does this happen? In the womb He is conceived, He grows little by little, and like me He follows the course of human growth. By what means? Through God's economy, not His Godhead; in the form of a slave, not as a master; in my own flesh, not in His divine essence.[45]

He increases little by little, mingling with humanity. He finds her full of sores, beaten down, oppressed by demons. And what does He do? He draws near to her. She sees Him and flees. He calls the magi, saying, "Why are you afraid? I am not a judge, but a physician. I have not come to judge the world, but to save the world."[46] Immediately He calls the magi. O new and paradoxical things! Immediately the firstfruits [of His coming] are wise men. The one upholding the universe lies in a manger; He who cares for all things is wrapped in swaddling bands. The temple is formed, and God dwells therein.

The magi come, and immediately they worship Him. The tax collector comes and becomes an evangelist; the prostitute comes and becomes a virgin; the Canaanite woman comes and enjoys His love for mankind. For this is what one does who ardently loves:[47] he does not demand an accounting for sins but forgives transgressions and offenses.

---

[45]Greek: "economy" (*oikonomia*), Godhead (*theotēs*), essence (*ousia*).
[46]Cf. Jn 12.47.
[47]Greek: *erōntos*.

And what does He do? He receives her and espouses her to Himself. And what does He give her? A signet ring. Of what sort? The Holy Spirit. For Paul says, *Now He who establishes us with you is God, who also has sealed us, giving us the earnest[48] of the Spirit* (2 Cor 1.21–22). The Spirit, then, He gives her.

Then He says, "Did I not plant you in the garden of Paradise?" She says, "Yes." "And how did you fall from there?" "The devil came and took me out of Paradise." "Yes, you were planted in Paradise, and he took you from there. Behold, I now implant you into Myself; I uphold and protect you. How is that? Because the devil does not dare to approach *Me*. And I do not lead you up to Heaven, for one greater than Heaven is here. I carry you within Myself—I, the Master of Heaven. The Shepherd carries you, and the wolf no longer comes. Or rather, I allow him to approach." And so the Lord carries our own nature, and the devil approaches and is defeated.

"I have implanted you within Myself." Hence, He says, "I am the Root; you are the branches."[49] And so He implanted her within Himself. But what else? She says, "I am a sinner, and unclean." He answers, "That does not matter to Me, for I am a physician. I know the vessel I created; I know how it got corrupted. It was at first a vessel of clay, but it became corrupted. I refashion it by the washing of regeneration [i.e., Baptism]; I deliver it to the fire [of the Holy Spirit in Chrismation]." Observe: He took dust from

---

[48]Greek: *arrabōn*.
[49]Cf. Jn 15.5.

the earth and made the man; He Himself fashioned him. Then the devil came and corrupted him. But then the Lord came, took him again, and remolded him, recasting him in Baptism, not allowing his body to remain but clay, but making him of harder earthenware.

He delivered the clay to the fire of the Spirit: *For He will baptize you in the Holy Spirit and fire* (Mt 3.11)—in water, to be remolded; and in fire, to be hardened. Therefore the prophet, speaking under inspiration from above, foretold: *Thou shalt dash them in pieces like a potter's vessel* (Ps 2.9). He did not say "as earthenware vessels" such as everyone possesses, for he was referring to vessels being fashioned by the potter on the wheel. Common vessels are made of clay, while ours are made of a harder substance. Speaking beforehand, therefore, of the remolding that occurs in Baptism, he says, *Thou shalt dash them in pieces like a potter's vessel*—meaning that He remolds and recasts them. For when I descend into the waters of Baptism, my form and nature[50] are refashioned—recast in the fire of the Spirit, becoming hard.

That these are not boastful words, listen to Job saying, *He made us as clay* (Job 10.9); while Paul says, *We have this treasure in hardened earthenware vessels* (2 Cor 4.7). Behold the strength of the earthen vessel—for it had been hardened not by regular fire, but by the fire of the Spirit. How was his vessel proven to be especially hard? *Five times I received forty lashes less one; three times I was beaten with rods; once I was stoned* (2 Cor 11.24–25), and yet his

---

[50]Greek: *schēma*.

earthen vessel was not shattered. *A day and a night in the deep* (v. 25). He was in the deep, yet his vessel was not dissolved; he suffered shipwreck, and the treasure was not lost; the ship was submerged, yet the cargo floated.

Having spiritual treasure

"Having the treasure." What kind of treasure? A plentiful supply of the Spirit, righteousness, sanctification, redemption. Of what sort? Tell me. *In the name of Jesus Christ, rise up and walk!* (Acts 3.6); *Aeneas, Jesus Christ heals you!* (Acts 9.34); *I say to you, you evil spirit, "Depart from him!"* (Acts 16.18).

Have you seen a treasure brighter than royal treasures? For what can a royal pearl accomplish, compared with the words of the apostle? Set a myriad of royal crowns upon one who is dead, and he will not be raised. But one word that came from the apostle brought back the [human] nature[51] that had rebelled, restoring it to its original condition.

"Having this treasure." O treasure that not only is preserved, but it preserves the house wherein it is stored!

Have you understood what I've said? Kings and rulers on the earth, when they have treasures, build and furnish great houses having strong walls, bars, doors, guards, and bolts in order for their treasures to be kept safe. Christ, however, did the opposite: He placed His treasure not in a vessel of stone, but in an earthen vessel. But if the treasure is great, why is its container weak? Yet the reason the

[51]Greek: *physin*.

vessel is weak is not that the treasure is great; for the treasure is not preserved by the vessel, but rather the treasure preserves the vessel.

Christ says, "I Myself deposit the treasure; who is, then, able to steal it? The devil has come, the world has come, multitudes have come; yet they have not stolen the treasure. The vessel was scourged, yet the treasure was not betrayed; the vessel was submerged in the sea, yet the treasure was not shipwrecked; the vessel died, but the treasure remains."

The earnest of the Spirit

He gave, therefore, the earnest[52] of the Spirit. Where are those who blaspheme the exaltedness of the Spirit? Be attentive: *The one establishing us with you in Christ is God, who also has given the earnest of the Spirit* (2 Cor 1.21–22). You all know that the earnest is a small portion of the whole. Listen to how this is. Someone goes to purchase a house of great value and says, "Give me a pledge, that I may have assurance." Or one goes to take a wife, arranging about the property and the dowry, and says, "Give me a pledge."

Give heed to what I'm saying. In the purchase of a slave, there is a pledge; and in all covenants there is one. Since, then, Christ makes a covenant with us (for He was about to take me as a bride), He also provides a dowry[53] for me— not of money, but of blood. This dowry that He gives me

[52]Greek: *arrabōna.*
[53]Greek: *proika.*

is the bestowal of good things that *eye has not seen, ear has not heard, neither have entered into the heart of man* (1 Cor 2.9). In the dowry He included immortality, praise with the angels, deliverance from death, freedom from sin, inheritance of the Kingdom (so great are the riches), righteousness, sanctification, deliverance from present things, and discovery of the things of the future.

Great was my dowry. Pay attention carefully. Observe what He does. He came to take the harlot—for I call her that, impure as she was, so that you will learn the fervent love of the Bridegroom.[54] He came, He took me, He gives me a dowry. He says, "I give you My wealth." How so? He says, "Did you lose Paradise? Take it back! Have you lost your beauty? Take it back! Take all these things." And yet my dowry was not given to me here.

Observe. This is the reason why He speaks of this dowry beforehand. He included in the dowry the resurrection of the body—immortality. Yet immortality does not always follow resurrection; the two are distinct. Many have arisen [from the dead] and yet have fallen again [in death], such as Lazarus and the bodies of the saints.[55] But in this case it's not like that, for the promise is of resurrection, immortality, a place with the choir of angels, meeting the Son in the clouds—*and so shall we ever be with the Lord* (1 Thess 4.17)—deliverance from death, freedom from sin, the complete annihilation of death.

---

[54]Greek: "harlot" (*pornēn*), "fervent love" (*erōta*).

[55]For Lazarus, see John 11; for the bodies of the saints, cf. Mt 27.52.

And of what sort of dowry is all of this? *Eye has not seen, ear has not heard, neither has entered into the heart of man what God has prepared for those who love*[56] *Him* (1 Cor 2.9). So do You give me good things that I do not know about? He says, "Yes—only be espoused to Me; only love[57] Me here and now." And why do You not give me the dowry here and now? "It will be given in full when you have come to My Father, when you have come into the royal palace. Did I not come to you, rather than your coming to Me? I came not so that you should remain here, but that I might take you and return [to Heaven]. So do not seek the dowry here—for here, everything is by hope; everything here is by faith."

So do You give me nothing here and now? He says, "Take the earnest,[58] so that you may trust Me concerning the things to come. Receive assurances, receive betrothal gifts." Therefore Paul says, *I have espoused you* (2 Cor 11.2).

As gifts of betrothal God has given us present blessings. These present gifts are an earnest [of future things], while the full dowry abides there [in the next world].[59] How so? I will tell you. Here I grow old; there I do not grow old. Here I die; there I do not die. Here I sorrow; there I do not sorrow. Here is poverty, disease, plots; there, nothing of the sort. Here is darkness and light; there, only light. Here are machinations; there, freedom from intrigue. Here, illness;

[56]Greek: *agapōsin*.
[57]Greek: *philei*.
[58]Greek: *arrabōna*.
[59]Greek: "earnest" (*arrabōn*), "dowry" (*proika*).

there, constant health. Here, life has an end; there, life has no end. Here is sinfulness; there, only righteousness, with no trace of sin. Here is envy; there, no such thing.

Someone says, "Give me these things now!" Be patient for now, so that your fellows may be saved; be patient. *The one who establishes us has given us the earnest.* What kind of earnest? The Holy Spirit—a supply of the Spirit.

Let me speak about the Spirit. He gave the "signet ring" to the apostles, saying, "Take this, and give it to everyone." Is the ring, then, distributed in portions? It is distributed, yet it remains undivided; it is distributed, yet it's never consumed.[60]

Let me teach you about the supply of the Spirit. Peter received, and Paul also received, the Holy Spirit. Paul went over the whole world, releasing sinners from their sins. And he restored the lame, clothed the naked, raised the dead, cleansed lepers, bridled the devil, strangled demons, conversed with God, planted churches, razed pagan temples to the ground, overturned heathen altars, destroyed vice, established virtue, made men into angels.

We were sinful and infirm as well.[61] And the earnest filled all the world. And when I say "all," I mean all that the sun shines upon—earth, sea, islands, mountains, valleys, and hills. Paul went all around as if on wings, with one mouth contending for the Faith—he, the tentmaker,

---

[60]Compare with the prayer at the fracture of the Gifts in the Liturgy of St John Chrysostom: "Broken and distributed is the Lamb of God: broken, yet not divided; ever eaten, yet never consumed, but sanctifying those who partake thereof."

[61]Literally, "We were all these things" (*tauta panta ēmen*).

who handled the craftsman's knife and sewed hides. Yet this trade of his was no hindrance to his virtue. For the tentmaker was stronger than demons; the ineloquent one was more philosophical than philosophers.

How was this? He had received the earnest; he bore the signet ring, and carried it about. Everyone saw that the King had espoused our nature. The demon saw this and withdrew. He saw the earnest, trembled, and retreated. He but saw Paul's garments and ran away.[62]

O the power of the Spirit! He gave authority not only to the soul, not only to the body, but even to clothing—and not only to clothing, but even to a shadow. For Peter went about, and his shadow made diseases flee; it expelled demons and raised the dead.[63] Paul went over the whole world, cutting away the thorns of ungodliness, casting about the seeds of godliness, like an excellent plowman handling the plow of sound teaching.

And to which peoples did he go? To Thracians, to Scythians, to Indians, to Maurians, to Sardinians, to Goths, to wild beasts; and he changed them all. How did all this happen? Through the earnest. What made him sufficient for all these things? The grace of the Spirit. Unskilled, ill-clothed, ill-shod, he had been given the earnest of the Spirit. Therefore he says, *And who is sufficient for these things?* (2 Cor 2.16) *But our sufficiency is from God, even He who has made us ministers of the New Covenant, not of the letter but of the Spirit* (2 Cor 3.5–6).

[62]See Acts 19.11–12.
[63]See Acts 5.15–16.

Behold what the Spirit has accomplished! He found the earth filled with demons, and made it Heaven. Do not meditate on present things [for now], but reflect on past things. For formerly there was lamentation; there were heathen altars everywhere—everywhere the smoke and fumes of heathen sacrifice, everywhere licentious rites and mysteries and sacrifices, everywhere demons inciting orgies, everywhere a citadel of the devil, everywhere fornication crowned with wreaths of "honor." And there was Paul, alone.

How was he not drowned? How was he not torn to pieces? How did he open his mouth? He entered the Thebaid and took men captive. He entered the royal palace and made the king a disciple.[64] He entered the court of justice, and the judge says to him, *You almost persuade me to become a Christian* (Acts 26.28); and he did become a disciple.

Paul entered into the prison and took the jailer captive.[65] He visited an island of barbarians and made a viper a means for his teaching.[66] He visited the Roman people and won over the Senate. He came to rivers; he came to desert places in all parts of the known world. There is no land or sea without a share in his righteous labors.

God gave the earnest of the signet ring; and having given the earnest, He says, "Some things I give you now, and others I promise." Therefore the prophet says, *At Thy*

[64]I.e., Sergius Paulus (Acts 13.4–12).
[65]Acts 16.16–34.
[66]Acts 28.1–6.

right hand stood the Queen, clothed in a vesture interwoven with gold (Ps 44.9). He does not mean an actual garment, but virtue. Therefore the Scripture says elsewhere, *How is it you have come here not wearing a wedding garment?* (Mt 22.12), referring not to being without an actual garment, but to living in fornication, in foul and unclean acts. As, then, foul raiment signifies sin, just so golden raiment signifies virtue. But this raiment belonged to the King; he is the one who gave it to her, for she was naked—naked and disfigured.

The garment interwoven with gold

At Thy right hand stood the Queen, clothed in a vesture interwoven with gold—speaking not of an actual vesture, but of virtue. He also did not say "of gold." Give heed, for the expression being used has great richness of meaning. He does not say "of gold," but "*interwoven* with gold." Listen with comprehension. A vesture "of gold" is one that is entirely made of gold; but one "*interwoven* with gold" is one that is partly of gold and partly of silk.

Why, then, did he say that the Bride wore a vesture not "of gold," but "interwoven with gold"? Pay careful heed. He is speaking of the Church in all her varied manifestations. For we do not all have just one condition of life— for instance, one lives in virginity, another in widowhood, another in dedicated devotion. So the garment of the Church represents the nature of the Church.

Our Master knew that if He provided only one path, many would shrink from it; hence He crafted many paths.

Is it not possible for you to pursue the path of virginity? Then take the path of a single marriage. Is a single not possible for you? Then be married for a second time. Is it not possible for you to live in abstinence? Then take the path of almsgiving. If not almsgiving? Then fasting. If not by this way? Then take that way! Or if not that, then this!

Hence the prophet spoke of a garment not "of gold," but "*interwoven* with gold." It could be of silk, or purple, or gold. You cannot be as gold? Then be as silk. I receive you, as long as you are clothed with an acceptable garment. So also Paul says, *If anyone builds upon this foundation, whether it be of gold, or silver, or precious stones* (1 Cor 3.12). You cannot be of precious stone? Then be of gold. You cannot be the gold? Then be the silver—just as long as you are in the foundation. Or as he says elsewhere, *There is one glory of the sun, another glory of the moon, another glory of the stars* (1 Cor 15.41). You cannot be the sun? Be the moon. You cannot be the moon? Be a star. You cannot be a great star? Be a little one—only be in the heavenly firmament.

You cannot live in virginity? Then get married and live in marital chastity—only in the Church. You cannot live without possessions? Then give alms—only abiding in the Church, only wearing a proper garment, only submitting to the Queen [i.e., the Church]. The raiment is interwoven with gold; it is variegated in composition.

I do not close off any path against you; for the abundance of virtues has made it easy to live according to the dispensation[67] of the King.

---

[67] Greek: *oikonomian.*

Clothed in a vesture interwoven with gold, wrought about with many colors (Ps 44.9). Her vesture is variegated; and if you will, unfold the depth of meaning in this expression, and behold the vesture interwoven with gold. For now there are some living in monasticism; others are abiding in solemn[68] matrimony, being not much inferior to the monastics. Some are only ever married once, and others live in widowhood in the flower of old age.

For what purpose is a garden? Why is it so variegated?—having diverse flowers, and trees, and many pearls. The stars are many, but there is only one sun; there are many ways of living, but only one Paradise. There are many temples, but only one Paradise—many temples, but only one Mother of them all.

In the body, there are the eyes, the fingers, and so on, which all comprise but one person. And while some parts are great, and others are less so, they all are crucial. The virgin has need of the married woman—for she is given birth through marriage, lest you despise marriage. The virgin is the root of marriage. Everything is bound together—the small with the great, and the great with the small.

At thy right hand stood the Queen, clothed in a vesture interwoven with gold. And then, *Hearken, O daughter!* The one leading the Bride to the Bridegroom's house says to her, "You are about to go to your Bridegroom who

---

[68]Greek: *semnon.*

surpasses you in His essence and in His nature.[69] I am the one leading you."

Hearken, O daughter! Did she immediately become His wife? No—for here there is nothing corporeal. For He espoused her as a wife, He loves[70] her as a daughter, He provides for her as a handmaid, He guards her as a virgin, He encloses her like a garden, He attends to her as His own member. As a head He provides for her; as a root He causes her to grow; as a shepherd He feeds her; as a Bridegroom He weds her; as a propitiation He pardons her; as a sheep He is sacrificed; as Bridegroom He preserves her in beauty; as a husband He provides for her welfare. Many are the meanings, so that we may enjoy even but a small part of the economy [of grace].

Hearken, O daughter, and behold! Look upon the things that are bridal, yet spiritual. *Hearken, O daughter!* At first, she was a daughter of demons, a daughter of the earth, unworthy of the earth; and now she has become the daughter of the King. This is what the One who loves her desired. For one who loves does not investigate the character of the beloved; one who loves does not notice her unseemliness. This is why it is called love, for often it loves[71] what is unlovely.

---

[69]Greek: "essence" (*ousian*), "nature" (*physin*). St John is continuing his theme here of Christ the Bridegroom coming to save humanity, which Chrysostom calls His "Bride."

[70]Greek: *philei*.

[71]Greek: *philei*. Preceding instances in this paragraph are all variants of *eros*: "the one loving" / "one who loves" (*erōn*, 3x), "love" (*erōs*).

This is what Christ did as well. He saw her unlovely (for I could not call her lovely), and He loved[72] her. And He makes her young, not having spot or wrinkle.[73] O what a Bridegroom!—making beautiful the unseemliness of His Bride!

The dowry has two parts

Hearken, O daughter! Hearken *and see!* He says two things: "Hearken" and "see"—two things that depend upon you: one on your eyes, and the other on your hearing. Since, then, her dowry depends upon hearing, and while some of you have been more acute in your understanding, let us tarry for those who are weaker (and I praise those of you who have anticipated the truth, while I make allowance for those who are following behind)—since, I say, her dowry depends upon hearing (and what is hearing? It is faith: *For faith comes by hearing* [Rom 10.17]—faith, not the actual experience of something), let us all clearly understand that, as I said before, God divided her dowry into two portions, giving some of it to the Bride as an earnest and promising the rest of it for the future.

So what has He given her already? He has given her forgiveness of sins, remission of punishment, righteousness, sanctification, redemption, the Body of the Master, the divine and spiritual table, resurrection of the dead. All these things the apostles had.

---

[72]Greek: *ērasthē.*
[73]See Eph 5.27.

Again, He bestowed some things and promised others. Of the first, there is experience and enjoyment thereof, while the rest depend on hope and faith.

Now listen! What else has He given already? Baptism and the Sacrifice [of Himself, in the Eucharist]. Of these, there is present experience. And now behold! What has He promised for the future? The resurrection, incorruptibility of the body, union with angels, being in chorus with the archangels, citizenship with Him [in Heaven], spotless life there, the good things *which eye has not seen, which ear has not heard, neither have entered into the heart of man, which God has made ready for those who love*[74] *Him* (1 Cor 2.9).

Understand what is being said; do not lose it! This is why I am laboring for you to perceive[75] it. Her dowry is divided into two portions—one for the present, and one for the future; one to be seen now, and one only to be heard about; one that has already been given, and one that is believed in; one that is already being experienced, and one to be enjoyed later; one for the present life, and one for after the resurrection. The former things you see already; the latter things you hear about.

Consider carefully, therefore, what He says to her, so that you do not suppose that she will only ever receive the former things—even though they are great and beyond telling, surpassing all understanding.

[74]Greek: *agapōsin*.
[75]Greek: *noēsēte*.

Hearken, O daughter, and behold! Hear about the future things, and observe the present things, so that you do not say, "Again in hope? Again in faith? Again, everything in the future?" Again, hear Christ saying, "Some things I give you now, while others I promise for the future. The latter indeed depend on hope, but receive the present things as pledges, as an earnest, as proof of what is to come. I promise you a Kingdom. Let the present things give you faith for the future things. Believe Me!"

Someone asks, "Do You promise me a Kingdom?" He replies, "Yes! Indeed, I have already given you the greater part—the Master of the Kingdom!" As Paul says, *For He spared not His own Son, but delivered Him up for us all; so how shall He not grace us with all things with Him?* (Rom 8.32).

"Do you give me the resurrection of the body?" "Yes! And I have already given you the greater part." "How so?" "Because I have already given you deliverance from sin." "How is that the greater part?" "Because sin brought forth death. I have strangled the parent, so shall I not also strangle the offspring? I have dried up the root; shall I not also destroy the fruit?"

Hearken, O daughter, and behold! She asks, "What am I to behold?" "The dead raised, lepers cleansed, the sea made calm, the paralytic restored, Paradise opened, loaves of bread abundantly appearing, sins dissolved, a lame man leaping, a thief becoming a citizen of Paradise, a tax collector becoming an evangelist, a harlot becoming more sober and modest[76] than a virgin.

---

[76]Greek: *semnoteran.*

"*Hearken, O daughter, and behold!* Hear about those things, and look upon these! Take proof [of the future things] from the present things, for I have given you pledges concerning the future things—things that are even better than the present things."

"And what else do you wish to say?" "These things are Mine. *Hearken, O daughter, and behold!* These things are My dowry for you!"

The Bride's contribution

And what does the Bride contribute? Let us see! The Bridegroom asks, "What, then, have you brought, so that you do not remain without a dowry?" She replies, "What do I have that I can present to You from heathen altars, from the steam [of heathen sacrifices], from demons? What do I have to offer? What?" He answers, "Only your resolution and your faith. *Hearken, O daughter, and behold!*"

The Bride then asks, "And what do You wish me to do?" "*Forget thy people.*" "What people?" "The demons, the idols, the smoke and steam and blood of pagan sacrifice. *And behold, forget thy people and thy father's house!* Leave your father, and come to Me! I have left My Father and I have come to you; but you will not leave your father?" (Now, when the word "leave" is used, referring to the Son [and the Father], do not take it to mean an actual leaving.)

The Bridegroom continues, "I condescended, I accommodated Myself to you, I took on flesh for you. That is the duty of the Bridegroom. So this is the duty of the Bride—that you should leave your parents, so that we may be wedded to each other. *Hearken, O daughter, and see, and incline thine ear; forget also thy people, and thy father's house."*

She asks, "And what will You give me, if I forget them?" He responds, "*And the king shall desire your beauty.* You have the Master as your Lover.[77] And since you have Him as your Lover, you also have the things that are His."

Physical beauty and noetic beauty

I hope you are able to comprehend what's being said—for the thought is subtle and profound, and I wish to stop the mouths of the Jews. So stretch forth your minds to me! But whether one understands or not, I will dig and till the soil. Now, when it is said, *Hearken, O daughter, and see, and incline thine ear; forget also thy people, and thy father's house. And the king shall desire thy beauty,* the Jew takes this to mean physical beauty—not noetic, but corporeal beauty.

So give heed! And let us learn what is physical beauty, and what is noetic beauty. There are two things—soul and body; and there is beauty of soul, and beauty of body. And what is beauty of body?—extended brows, smiling eyes, blushing cheeks, rosy lips, a straight neck, flowing hair, tapering fingers, upright stature, a fair and blooming complexion. Now, does this bodily beauty come naturally, or from one's choice? Confessedly, it comes from nature.

Be heedful, so that you may learn the thoughts of philosophers. This beauty, whether of the countenance, or the eyes, or the hair, or the brows—does it come from nature,

[77]Greek: *erastēn.*

or from choice? It's evident that it comes from nature. The unlovely woman, even if she tries to beautify herself in countless ways, is not able to become lovely in body; for natural conditions are fixed, confined by limits that cannot be crossed over. The lovely woman is always lovely, even if she does not make an effort to beautify herself, while the unlovely woman is unable to make herself beautiful, just as the lovely one cannot become unlovely. Why is this? Because these things come from nature.

Have you seen corporeal beauty? Now let us turn inward, to the beauty of the soul. Let the handmaid approach the mistress; let us turn to the soul. Look upon that beauty—or rather, hear about it, for it cannot be seen, since it is invisible. So hear about that beauty.

What, then, is beauty of soul? Prudence, gentleness, almsgiving, love, brotherly kindness, tender affection,[78] obedience to God, fulfillment of the law, righteousness, contrition of heart. These things characterize beauty of soul. And they are not from nature, but from free choice. Someone not having these things is able to gain them; and someone having them, if he is negligent, loses them.

As I was saying about the body—that someone who is unlovely cannot become beautiful—now about the soul I say the opposite: that an unlovely soul can become beautiful. What could have been more unlovely than Paul's soul when he was a blasphemer, and insolent? And what could be more beautiful than his soul when he said, *I have fought*

[78]Greek: "prudence" (*sōphrosynē*), "love" (*agapē*), "brotherly kindness" (*philadelphia*), "tender affection" (*philostorgia*).

the good fight, I have finished the race, I have kept the faith
(2 Tim 4.7)? What was more unlovely than the soul of the
thief? Yet what became more lovely when he heard, *Truly,*
I say to you, today you will be with Me in Paradise (Lk
23.43)? What was more unlovely than the soul of the tax
collector when he plundered? Yet what was more lovely
than when he made his commitment to follow Jesus?

Behold how you cannot change physical loveliness,
since it's not from one's choice, but from nature. But spiritual beauty comes from one's own moral choice.

You have now received the teaching. Of what, again?
That beauty of soul comes from obedience to God. For if
an unlovely soul obeys God, it lays aside its unloveliness
and becomes beautiful. "Saul, Saul! Why do you persecute
Me?" And he replied, "Who are You, Lord?" "I am Jesus."
And he obeyed; and his obedience made his unlovely
soul beautiful.[79] And again, Jesus says to the tax collector, "Come, follow Me." And the tax collector arose and
became an apostle, and his unlovely soul became beautiful. How so? Through obedience. Again, Jesus says to the
fishermen, *Come after Me, and I will make you become*
fishers of men (Mt 4.19). And through their obedience,
their minds became beautiful.

So let us see what kind of beauty is spoken of in the
psalm, *Hearken, O daughter, and see, and incline thine*
ear; forget also thy people, and thy father's house. And the
king shall desire thy beauty. What kind of beauty will He
desire? That of the soul. And how does she demonstrate

[79]See Acts 9.1–18.

this? Because she forgot [her own people]. The Psalmist says, "Hearken, and forget." These things are from one's free will. "Hearken," he says. Someone unlovely in body listens, yet her physical unloveliness is not removed. But if a sinful woman, unlovely in her soul, listens and obeys, she will see what manner of spiritual beauty is bestowed upon her.

Since, then, the Bride's unloveliness was not physical, but moral (for she had transgressed, not being obedient to God), the Bridegroom leads her to another remedy, and says to her, "You were unlovely—not by nature, but by your moral choice. Then you became beautiful in soul through your obedience."

Hearken, O daughter, and see, and incline thine ear; forget also thy people, and thy father's house. And the king shall desire thy beauty. So that you might learn that this word "beauty" is not referring to anything physical, do not think of eye, or nose, or mouth, or neck, but of godliness, faith, love[80]—things that are within. *All the glory of the king's daughter is within* (Ps 44.14).

For all these things let us give thanks to God, the Giver; for to Him alone belong glory, and honor, and might, unto the ages of ages. Amen.

---

[80]Greek: *agapēn.*

Oration on the Relics

A note on the text

St John is ecstatic that young Empress Eudoxia entered the Great Church in Constantinople in the middle of the night and went up to a chest placed there, containing the relics of three martyrs, which had recently arrived in the city, having been sent as a gift, most likely by Bishop Vigilius of Trent, in northern Italy.[1] She then accompanied the relics in a grand procession, along with "the entire city and its magistrates," to a martyrium—a martyrs' shrine—located some nine miles outside the capital in the suburb of Drypia.

Dawn has broken when he begins his homily, in which he extols the merits of the martyrs, the great gain that comes from venerating them and their ever grace-bearing relics, and the wonderful piety of the Christ-loving empress.

[1]See Kelly, *Golden Mouth,* 139–41.

This event occurred most likely in the year 400, probably not too long after Emperor Arcadius' wife Eudoxia was officially made empress, on January 9 of that year. At this point St John and the empress were still on very good terms; he still had firm confidence that they would be able, through such events as this, to work together to greatly strengthen the spiritual life of the capital city. He may have even hoped that he could be a kind of father-figure for her, since she was only about twenty-three years old, and had been orphaned as a young girl, and was now living in a foreign land (she was daughter of the Gothic consul Bautho, and had been raised in faraway Frankish territory). By this point John was about fifty-three years old.

St John's words of glowing, heartfelt praise for Empress Eudoxia, "more radiant than the moon," expressed here make it all the more poignant that within about three years she would turn so decidedly against him that she played a major role in having him sent into exile after the infamous Synod of the Oak in September of 403.

Oration on the Relics[2]

What can I say? What shall I speak forth? I'm leaping with joy; I'm beside myself with an ardor better at this moment than temperance! I'm flying, dancing, floating on air, so intoxicated am I with spiritual pleasure.

What can I say? What should I speak about? About the strength of the martyrs? About the eager desire of the city? About the zeal of the empress? About the gathering of the magistrates? About the disgrace of the devil? The defeat of the demons? The nobility of the Church? The power of the cross? The miracles of the Crucified One? The glory of the Father? The grace of the Spirit? The spiritual pleasure of all the people? The leaping for joy of the city? The assemblies of monks? The choirs of virgins? The ranks of clergy? The exertion and effort of the laity—both slaves and free,

---

[2]PG 63:467–472; for another modern English translation, see Wendy Mayer and Pauline Allen, *John Chrysostom* (London: Routledge, 2000), 86–92.

both those ruling and those being ruled, both the poor and the rich, both foreigners and citizens of our city?

How timely and fitting it is to speak about all these things! For *Who shall speak of the mighty acts of the Lord? Who shall make all His praises to be heard?* (Ps 105.2)

Women who stay in their chambers and are softer than wax have come out of their enclosed dwellings; and copying the eagerness of the strongest of the men, they have traversed such a long distance by foot. And not only young women, but old ones besides; and neither the weakness of their nature, nor the delicacy of their manner of living, nor any of the vanity surrounding them were obstacles to their eagerness. And magistrates also left behind their carriages and staff-bearers and bodyguards, and have intermixed with the common folk.

Yet why is it needful to speak of women and magistrates when the one who wears the royal diadem and is clothed in the royal purple is here—she who for the entire journey could not bear even for a moment to be separated from the relics? Rather, like a handmaiden, she followed closely behind the holy relics, touching the casket and the veil covering it. And trampling upon all human vanity, she has allowed herself to be seen in this place by everyone— she whom all the eunuchs serving in the imperial palace do not have the right to see. Indeed, her yearning for the martyrs, the tyranny and flame of her love for them,[3] has persuaded her to tear off all masks, and to show forth with unrestrained enthusiasm her zeal for the holy martyrs.

[3]Greek: "yearning" (*pothos*), "love" (*agapēs*).

I am reminded now of the blessed David, who likewise was clothed in a purple robe and was crowned with a royal diadem, having the scepter of authority over the Hebrew people. And when he brought up the Ark, he laid aside all those symbols of power and leapt and danced, greatly cavorting and dancing like a child. And through his leaping he made evident the pleasure he had in that celebration.[4]

If David was impelled to show forth such enthusiasm for the shadow and the type, how much more for *grace and truth* (Jn 1.14)? For this chest that the empress has brought here is of much more value than the one David brought. For hers does not have tablets of stone within, but spiritual tablets, blossoming with grace—gleaming gifts, bones reflecting the rays of the sun. Or rather, they send forth lightning flashes that are even more brilliant than the sun. For demons do not suffer harm when they behold the rays of the sun, but they are unable to bear the brilliance that bursts forth from these relics. For it blinds them, and compels them to run and flee far away. So great even is the power of the ashes of the saints that it does not simply remain within the casket but extends far beyond it, repelling the unclean powers and sanctifying with great abundance those who approach them with faith.

This is precisely why the Christ-loving empress kept following so closely behind the relics, constantly reaching

---

[4]It is very interesting that St John assumes that his listeners know he is talking here about King David bringing the Ark of the Covenant up into Jerusalem (1 Chron 15.27–29).

out and touching them, absorbing the blessing, and hence becoming a teacher of all others about this beautiful spiritual commerce, instructing everyone to draw from this fountain that is ever drained but never emptied. Just as waters bubbling up from a spring do not just remain pooled up at that spot but overflow and spread forth widely, so the grace of the Spirit that accompanies these bones and dwells with the saints extends towards others who follow the relics with faith, as the grace flows from soul to body, and from body to clothing, and from clothing to shoes, and from shoes even to one's shadow. That is exactly how it suffused not only the bodies of the apostles, but also their handkerchiefs and aprons.[5] And not only their handkerchiefs and aprons, but also Peter's shadow performed deeds more powerful than those of the living.[6]

In former times, the sheepskin placed upon Elisha's body brought him a twofold gift; for it was not only his body that was filled with grace, but also his clothing.[7] And the same with the Three Youths, for the nature of the flames not only respected their bodies, but also their shoes.[8] And with Elisha, the grace did not come to an end even after he died; for death was thwarted when another corpse was thrown into the prophet's grave.[9]

[5] Acts 19.11–12.

[6] Acts 5.15–16.

[7] 3 Kingdoms LXX (1 Kgs) 19.19 and 4 Kingdoms LXX (2 Kgs) 2.12–14.

[8] Dan 3.27.

[9] 4 Kingdoms LXX (2 Kgs) 13.21.

And so it has happened today; for as the relics were being carried, demons were bursting into flame. Cries and shrieks of lament went up everywhere, as the ray of light leapt forth from the bones, utterly consuming the phalanx of opposing demons.

So I am leaping and flying for joy, because this deserted place has been made a city, with the city now emptied; and because today you have shown forth the wealth of our Church. Behold so many sheep, and nowhere a wolf! So many grapevines, and nowhere a thistle! So much wheat, and nowhere tares! A sea stretched from the city right up to our present location—a sea without waves, having no shipwrecks, free from craggy headlands, sweeter than all honey, with waters more drinkable than the purest water.

And one would not be amiss in calling this sea a river of fire. For throughout the night, everyone with their lamps, being packed tightly together, stretching in a continuous line all the way to this martyrium, presented the vision of a fiery river to those watching.

And that was in the night! Now that daylight has come, other lamps are shining. For while the sunlight is now obscuring those lamps and making them dim, the light in the minds of each of you is becoming brighter; for the fire of your eagerness is warmer than those lights that were seen in the night. Each one of you carried a double lamp— the one of fire in the night, and the one of your zeal both in the night and in the day.

And yet, I would not even call what has passed night- time, for it rivaled the day, bearing up all you sons of light and revealing you to be brighter than the myriad of stars, along with the morning star. Just as those who are inebriated make the day night, so those who with watchfulness celebrate all-night vigils make the night day. This explains why all night long the prophetic hymn was chanted, which says, *The night shall be light to my delight. For the darkness shall not be dark to thee, and the night shall shine like the day; its darkness and its light are both alike to thee* (Ps 138.11–12).

For didn't this past night become brighter than any day, with everyone leaping with such an abundance of joy, having such profound spiritual joy, with such multitudes of people pouring out and flooding both the road and the marketplace? Indeed, none of the pavement could be seen, so densely packed together were the people standing on it. And for the entire course of the procession, you all formed a single continuous golden chain, a single river flowing along with much fervor.

Gazing up at the heavens, we beheld the moon and the stars in the midst; and looking out upon the multitude of the faithful, we beheld the empress being borne along in the midst, more radiant than the moon. For just as the "stars" here below are better than those above, so this "moon" is more brilliant than that one. And why is this? Is that moon as great as a soul in such a high position of authority being adorned with such profound faith?

Which quality of hers should we admire first? Her zeal, hotter than fire? Her faith, stronger than steel? Her contrite mind and humility, because of which she put aside all her imperial insignia? For casting off crowns and other imperial accoutrements, along with all the vanity that abundantly surrounds those things, she has clothed herself in the robe of humility instead of the royal purple. And through this she shines all the more radiantly.

There have been many, many empresses, who shared not only the royal stole and the crowns, but also the imperial glory. But the humble adornment of this one alone has become exceptional; this trophy belongs to her alone. For she alone among empresses has conducted martyrs in procession with such great honor, with such great zeal and piety, mingling with the multitude, dispensing with her entire retinue of servants and bodyguards, and regarding as nothing the heights of her office and regal way of life.

This is how she has benefited the people no less than the martyrs have. Just as everyone was looking towards the relics, so also they all—both rich and poor—were gazing at her attentiveness, watching her tightly holding onto the bones for so long a journey, neither growing weary nor turning aside, but hanging onto the casket.

Because of all of this, we are not ceasing to call you blessed[10]—and not only we ourselves, but all future generations also, since what has happened here will be heard about to all the ends of the inhabited world, everywhere on earth that the sun shines. The people in our time will hear about it, as well as those coming afterwards. No epoch will consign what has happened here to oblivion. For God Himself is spreading with much acclaim the

[10]Here he is addressing the empress.

news about these things everywhere in the world and to all future generations. If He made the action of a prostitute to be known to the ends of the world, establishing it as an immortal memorial of her,[11] how much more will He not allow to be forgotten the work of a decorous, solemn, and prudent woman who has displayed such great piety in the empire!

Rather, everyone will call you blessed, as one who gave hospitality to the saints, as a patroness of the churches, as one equal to the apostles in zeal. For though you received a feminine nature, it is still possible for you to rival the apostles in good works, too. After all, there was that Phoebe, who welcomed the teacher of the world into her home and became his patroness,[12] and yet she was a woman, sharing the same nature as yourself. Yet she was so illustrious that he, a saint who was worthy of the heavens and was greater than all the apostles, extolled her, saying, *She has become the patroness of many, including myself* (Rom 16.2).

Priscilla, too, received a feminine nature, yet that was no impediment to her being acclaimed and her memory being immortalized.[13] And there was at that time a large "choir" of women sharing in the apostolic life.

And we are not missing the mark in now numbering you with them, for you are a harbor for all the churches, and you have used the present kingdom to gain the

[11]See Mt 26.6–13.

[12]He is referring here to her patronage of St Paul.

[13]See Acts 18.1–3, 24–26; Rom 16.3.

coming Kingdom. You have corrected churches, you have honored priests, you have put an end to heretical error. And you have welcomed martyrs, not with material hospitality, but with your heart; not with a tent, but with your intention—or rather, with both tent and intention.

Miriam, too, once led forth the people while following Joseph's bones and sang a song.[14] She did this after the Egyptians had been drowned; you did so while demons were being choked. She did it after Pharaoh had drowned; you did so after the devil had been brought down. She did it wielding cymbals; you did so with your mind and soul, resounding louder than a trumpet. She did it because the Jews had been freed; you did so because the Church is being crowned.

She led forth a single nation, having one language; you have led forth a myriad of peoples, having different languages. For you have led forth for us a myriad of choruses—some in the language of the Romans, some in the tongue of the Syrians, others in the tongues of barbarians, and some in the Greek language—all striking up the Psalms of David. One can see a variety of ethnic groups and different choirs all having a single lyre, so to speak—that of David—and crowning you with their prayers.

Missing from the cheer of this festival is the God-loving emperor, who along with you pulls the plow of piety. But it's through your good sense that this has happened—keeping him home today, while promising that he will be here tomorrow. It was in accordance with your wisdom

---

[14]Ex 15.20–21.

that you spread the celebration across two days. Otherwise, with the addition of a multitude of horses and armed soldiers, the festival might have been thrown into great confusion, grieving especially the virgins, elderly women, and old men.

If they had both been present today, the festival would now be coming to an end. But, in order to ensure peacefulness today, as well as to lavishly extend the celebration with the addition of another day, she has divided the liturgical duty[15] with him. So she is here today, and she has announced that he will be here tomorrow. Just as she shares the imperial office with him, so also they share in piety; she does not allow him to be without a share in her good works, but in everything she takes him as her partner.

So, since this spiritual celebration is being extended through tomorrow, let us again display the same zeal, so that just as today we have seen the empress who loves Christ with the city, tomorrow we will behold the God-beloved emperor, present along with the army, and offering to God the same sacrifice—namely, that of piety, zeal, and faith.

And taking the holy martyrs as partners in our prayers, let us pray for the imperial couple to have long life, a ripe old age, children, and grandchildren. And beyond all this, let us pray that their zeal may be increased and their piety may be enriched; and in this way they may conclude this present life, so that through the incorruptible ages they

---

[15]Greek: *leitourgian.*

may reign together unto the Only-Begotten Son of God. *For if we persevere*, it says, *we shall reign together with Him* (2 Tim 2.12).

May we attain these eternal good things—may we all be worthy of them!—by the grace and love for mankind of our Lord Jesus Christ, to whom be glory, along with the Father and the Holy Spirit, now and ever, and unto ages of ages. Amen.

Homily on His Return from Asia

A note on the text

Sometime during Great Lent in 402, after about four years of ministry as archbishop of Constantinople, St John made a pastoral visit to Ephesus, in the Roman province of Asia, in southwestern Asia Minor. The main reason for his journey there was to investigate charges of simony—the crime of buying church office—brought against a number of bishops in that region. That business kept him away from the capital for about three and a half months.

In this sermon, the first one he preached upon his return to Constantinople, St John rejoices that he finds his flock in such excellent condition, as he amply describes. Indeed, his praises for his people comprise the bulk of the homily.

It was only a little more than a year later that St John was condemned at the infamous Synod of the Oak, where one of the principal accusations against him was that in going to Ephesus and conducting such serious Church business there, he had illegally invaded the territory of another major bishopric. In point of fact, the extent of Constantinople's ecclesiastical authority over Ephesus was unclear in St John's day.

Homily on His
Return from Asia[1]

Moses was a great servant of God, the head of the prophets, who led the way through the sea, who controlled the
air,[2] who set manna on the table in the wilderness. He was
cast forth by the one who bore him and was saved by her
enemy—for his mother set him out [in the basket] and
the Egyptian woman gathered him up and raised him. He
was nurtured in Egypt, but his citizenship was in Heaven.[3]
He erected a great trophy over the Egyptians; he made the

---

[1]Greek text in Antoine Wenger, "L'homélie de Saint Jean Chrysos-
tome «A Son Retour d'Asie,»" *Revue des études byzantines* 19 (1961):
110–123; another modern English translation may be found in Wendy
Mayer and Pauline Allen, *John Chrysostom* (London: Routledge, 2000),
99–103.

[2]Probably having in mind the various airborne plagues that struck
the Egyptian nation through Moses' agency—dog-flies, hail, and lo-
custs (Ex 8–10).

[3]See Phil 3.20.

sea to stand fast; he split a rock in two; he conversed with God as with a friend.

This man, who was so outstanding, after leaving his people for only forty days,[4] returned to find them in a state of rebellion and lawlessness. Yet I, who left you for not just forty or fifty or a hundred days, now find you well-disciplined, displaying Christian philosophy and even greater godliness. For you are more sensible and prudent than they were.

This is why Moses, upon descending from the mountain, plaited an accusation against Aaron; while I, as I stand now among you, am weaving accolades and plaiting crowns of victory for you. For where there is transgression, indictments follow; whereas righteous deeds bring praises and crowns. Therefore, even though I spent much time away from you, I had much confidence in your good will, your love, your faith, and your mindfulness, knowing that you, the flock I am married to, eagerly strive to be sensible and prudent.

This is how things are on the outside as well. For a man who has an intemperate wife does not even allow her to peep outside the house; and if by necessity he has to make a trip away from home, he makes every effort to return home quickly, driven by suspicion as if pricked by a thorn. Whereas the man who has a sensible and prudent wife takes his time when he is away, regarding his wife's good character as sufficient to guarantee her security.

---

[4]Referring to the time Moses spent on Mt Sinai receiving revelations from the Lord, including the gift of the Ten Commandments.

This is what Moses and I experienced: with him, since he left behind an intemperate wife—the synagogue—God pressed him, saying, *Arise! Go back down! The people have transgressed the law* (Ex 32.7); but with me, I received no such command; I could continue ministering to those in need without concern. For it's not the healthy who have need of a doctor, but those who have afflictions.[5]

If I did forsake you for a while, it was not out of contempt for you, but to enhance your riches. For the things that were set aright through me—or rather, through grace—while I was away redound as a crown for you. This is why I am rejoicing, leaping for joy, flying with pleasure.

Yes, I'm rejoicing, but I cannot explain how great my joy is. What, then, is to be done, so that you may learn how great is my joy? I summon your conscience as witness; for you know from what you have experienced upon seeing me how it is with me, being convinced by the very sight of me.

For if, for you, the appearance of just one man has caused such delight for so many people, how much more delight is being aroused in my soul through my beholding so many people whom I love?[6] For with Jacob, the sight of just one man, his son Joseph, brought such joy that the old man was rejuvenated;[7] while with me, I have beheld

---

[5]See Mt 9.12.

[6]Greek: *pothoumenōn*.

[7]Referring to Joseph's reunion with his father in Goshen, as Jacob was on his way to Egypt (Gen 46.28–30).

not just one man, but a myriad of men one after another—indeed, the entire populace!

It's on account of these things that I rejoice—that I have received back my paradise, a paradise better than the one of old. For there, the serpent was present setting snares; while here, Christ is instructing us in the Mysteries. There, Eve was working deception; here, the Church is being crowned. There, Adam was deceived; here, the populace is being publicly acclaimed. There, there were differing sorts of trees; here, there are many diverse spiritual gifts. In Eden, there were trees that withered; here, in the Church, the trees never cast off their fruit.

And what is astonishing, this garden not only protects its plants, but *transforms* them. For if I find a thistle, I work it into a grapevine; and if I find an olive tree that is not bearing fruit, I work it into a fruit-bearing tree. Such is the nature of the soil here.

Because of all this, I rejoice and leap for joy. But just because I'm rejoicing does not mean I will skip over my defense for my absence. So, beloved, since I was away for such a long time, receive my defense. If you had sent a slave somewhere, would you not demand an account from him upon his return—asking, "Where did you spend your time? Where did you squander so much time?"

I, too, am a slave—a slave to your love for me. You purchased me, not by casting down silver, but by showing forth your love.[8] I rejoice in this slavery! May I never be loosed from it! For this slavery is better than a crown; this

---

[8]Greek: *agapēn.*

slavery procures the Kingdom of Heaven; this slavery is better than freedom; this slavery prepares for me a throne at the Last Judgment. And this slavery is not a matter of compulsion, but of free choice.

Who would not gladly serve you as a slave, since you are such mad lovers?[9] If I had a heart of stone, you have made it softer than wax.

What can I say about the love[10] you have demonstrated?—the mania, the frenzy of yesterday, the shouting in the marketplace? You sanctified the air; you made the city a church. I was held in honor, yet it was God who was welcomed. Heretics were put to shame; the Church was crowned; you were publicly acclaimed. For it's smooth sailing for the Church when the root is bound with the branches, when the shepherd dwells securely with his flock.

I returned and received good news.[11] Of what sort? That you trampled upon heretics; that you convinced lawbreakers to receive Baptism. It was not in vain that I said that while her husband was away, the sensible and prudent wife confounded her would-be adulterers; that with the shepherd away, the flock chased away the wolves; that without the captain, the sailors brought the ship home safely; that without the general, the soldiers raised up the trophy; that without their teacher, the students progressed; that without their father, the children grew big

[9]Greek: *manikois ousin erastais*.
[10]Greek: *pothon*.
[11]Greek: *euangelia*.

and strong. Yet it was not really without their father—for your good deeds are my crown, my cause for boasting.

"But," you say, "we desired to celebrate Pascha with you." If this is most especially the reason you were also upset upon seeing me, I will make my defense about that, even though if the father welcomed back his senseless son without demanding an account from him, and immediately enfolded him in his embrace,[12] so much more it ought to be that way when the children welcome back their father.

"But still," you say, "we wanted to celebrate Pascha with you." All right—I will justify myself on this account. So, you wanted to celebrate Pascha with me? There is nothing preventing you! Celebrate Pascha with me today! Will we then celebrate two Paschas today? No, for it will be the same Pascha over and over. Just as the sun always rises, yet we do not see many different suns but the same one rising every day, so also Pascha is always being celebrated, yet it is always one and the same Pascha that is being celebrated.

The Jewish festivals and ours are not the same. I am not enslaved to a place, and I am not constrained by certain moments in time. *For as often as you eat this Bread and drink of this Cup, you proclaim the death of the Lord* (1 Cor 11.26). So let us proclaim today the death of the Lord. For then it was a feast day, and today it is also.

And wherever there is love,[13] it is a feast. Even, children, when you lose a father, it is a feast—for that also is a

[12]See Lk 15.11–24.
[13]Greek: *agapē*.

festival of love. *For God so loved the world that He gave His Only-Begotten Son for us* (Jn 3.16).

"But," you say, "many were baptized without you at Pascha." And what of that? The grace was not lessened; the gift was not defective. While they were not baptized in my presence, they were baptized in the presence of Christ. Surely it's not a man who does the baptizing! A man lends his right hand, but it is God who moves that hand.

Do not be double-minded about the grace, beloved. And why not? I'm telling you: Baptism is a gift.

Pay very careful attention to what I'm saying. If you submit a petition to the emperor and receive it back with his signature on it, you don't get worked up about what sort of pen he used, or what sort of paper or ink; you only look to see that he has indeed signed it. It's the same with Baptism, wherein the paper is one's conscience, the pen is the priest's tongue, and the hand is the grace of the Spirit. So whether it's my hand or that of another, the Hand that writes is the same.

We are servants, not despots. Even Paul was a servant; as he says, *Let a man consider us to be as servants of Christ, as stewards of the Mysteries of God* (1 Cor 4.1). And also, *For what do you have that you did not receive?* (1 Cor 4.7). If I have something, I have received it; and if I have received it, it's not mine, but it is a gift belonging to the One who gave it.

Beloved, do not then be in any doubt. When grace was perfected, the place was not a hindrance, even if it happened on a ship. Philip baptized [the Ethiopian eunuch] on a road;[14] Paul baptized in prison;[15] Christ led the thief into Paradise.

Because of all this I rejoice, I take delight, and I ask for your prayers—with which I left you, and with which I have now returned. I journeyed by sea, but your love[16] made the waters calm. I did not enter the ship without you; I did not disembark for overnight lodging without you; I did not enter a city or a church without you. For even though we were separated from you in body, we were bound together with you in love.[17]

Even while at sea I saw your church as unwavering; for such is our love, that it knows no constriction. When I would enter a church and stand beside the altar, all the while I would be remembering your church. And I would send up prayers, saying, "Lord, hold in trust the church You entrusted to me. I am not present, but You are—You who led me there." And now I say to Him, "You have brought to pass, by Your grace, more than I asked."

I asked that He would watch over you, and He has fulfilled that request. The great crowd here is a witness—such luxuriant grapevines, and nowhere any thistles; such sheep, and nowhere any wolves. And if there be a wolf, he is transformed and becomes a sheep. God Himself watched over you; He Himself brought me back to you. Your prayers restored me to health, and this I say every day.

[14]Acts 8.26–39.
[15]Acts 16.25–33.
[16]Greek: *agapē*.
[17]Greek: *agapē*.

My journey has crowned your city. Your love for me was evident before this, but it was not clear to everyone. Only those who loved me knew it before; but now this time of separation has proven it to all. People were constantly coming into Asia and telling me, "You have set the city on fire!"

Love usually withers from time apart; but your love for me has increased during this time of separation! It did not succumb to forgetfulness; it became inflamed all the more!

So I ask that you love me in the same way, now that I have returned. This is my treasure; this is my wealth. This is why I seek your prayers, since they form a wall of security around me.

Don't say to me, "But I am a layperson; how can I pray for a priest?" Listen to the Scriptures saying, *There was abundant prayer offered up by the church* (Acts 12.5), and Peter's chains were loosed. It was prayer that loosed Paul's silence,[18] that bridled the lions,[19] that muzzled the whale,[20] that opened Paradise [to the thief].[21] Prayer opened wide the vaults of Heaven,[22] the prayer of Cornelius penetrated

---

[18]Possibly referring to the prayer the Church of Antioch made before sending Paul and Barnabas on their first missionary journey (cf. Acts 13.1–3), which initiated Paul's preaching to the world far beyond the confines of Antioch.

[19]See Dan 6.17–23 LXX.

[20]Jonah 2.1–11.

[21]Lk 23.42.

[22]3 Kingdoms LXX (1 Kgs) 18.41–45.

the Heavens,[23] and the prayer of the tax collector made him righteous.[24]

So I ask this from you for my own security. And furthermore, I ask for this—that God, upon receiving your prayers, would grace you with an abundance of blessings, both in the present age, and in the age to come, in Christ, to whom be glory unto the ages. Amen.

[23] Acts 10.1–4.
[24] Lk 18.9–14.

Homily before
His First Exile

A note on the text

Many forces and factors coalesced to result in St John's being deposed from his position as archbishop of Constantinople at a "kangaroo court" engineered and led by his nemesis, Archbishop Theophilus of Alexandria, in a suburb of Chalcedon, in late September of 403. Known as the Synod of the Oak, it was comprised of thirty-six bishops, twenty-nine of whom had come from Egypt with Theophilus when Theophilus himself was summoned to stand trial for apparently holding Origenistic beliefs considered to be heretical. But amazingly, by ingratiating himself with Empress Eudoxia—who resented John's frequent preaching against the luxury and ostentation of the wealthy—and by drawing upon animosity against John held by a number of bishops and priests who thought he was too strict in his expectations of their clerical duties, and too intransigent in his personality, Theophilus was able, incredibly, to "turn the tables" and bring John to trial instead of himself!

This is the homily that John preached two days after his condemnation and exile were announced to the citizens of the city. One of his biographers, Donald Attwater, vividly describes the scene, and the sermon:

> For three days the city was in an uproar. Theophilus had gotten a majority of the clergy around to his side, but most of the common people were wholeheartedly behind their archbishop. They demonstrated in the streets, they picketed the episcopal house and cathedral, and guarded Chrysostom in a body as he passed from one to the other.
>
> On the second day he preached to a congregation packed nearly to suffocation. It was a bold address, not calculated to calm the people or gratify the authorities, but it was Chrysostom in his essence: the Christian shepherd standing up against injustice before the kings of the earth, not fearful for the effect of his words because they were words of truth, welcoming the will of God and trusting in his Christ, ready for all that might come, since "the good shepherd gives his life for his sheep."[1]

On the following day, the archbishop gave himself into the hands of armed guards, who took him into exile that night.

[1] Donald Attwater, *St John Chrysostom: Pastor and Teacher* (London: Harvill Press, 1959), 121–22.

Homily before
His First Exile[2]

Many are the waves, and fierce are the storms, but we do not fear. Neither are we being drowned, for we are standing on the Rock. Let the sea rage; it is not able to shake the Rock! Let the waves rise up; they are not strong enough to sink the ship of Christ!

What do we have to fear? Tell me! Death? *To me, to live is Christ, and to die is gain* (Phil 1.21). Exile? Tell me! *The earth is the Lord's, and the fullness thereof* (Ps 23.1). Confiscation of property? *We brought nothing into this world; and it is evident that we can take nothing out of it* (1 Tim 6.7).

[2]Greek text: PG 52:427–32.

For me, the things the world fears are easily despised; and the things the world cherishes are easily scorned. I do not fear poverty; neither do I desire wealth. I do not fear death; neither do I pray to live, unless it would be for your benefit.

Therefore I call to remembrance your love, and I beseech you to take courage. Nothing is able to separate us. For what God has joined together, man is not able to split apart. For if concerning a wife and a husband He says, *For this reason a man shall leave his father and mother, and shall be joined unto his wife, and they shall be one flesh* (Gen 2.24); and, *What God has yoked together, let not man split asunder* (Mt 19.5); if you cannot split apart a marriage, how much less are you strong enough to tear apart the Church of God?[3]

You wage against her, but you are not able to injure what you are warring against. You are making me more illustrious, while you dissolve your own strength through fighting against me. *It is hard for you to kick against the pricks* (Acts 9.5; 26.14). You are not blunting the pricks; rather, they are bloodying your feet. The waves are not vanquishing the Rock; rather, the Rock is reducing the waves to foam.

Nothing is stronger than the Church, O man! Cease your attack against her, lest you lose all your strength. Do not wage war against Heaven! If you wage war against men, either you are victorious or you are defeated. But

[3]St John has shifted at this point from speaking to his flock to speaking to his enemies.

if you wage war against the Church, she will defeat you without weapons; for God is stronger than everything. *Are we not provoking the Lord to jealousy? Are we stronger than He?* (1 Cor 10.22). God has built His Church; who dares to put forth his hand to shake her?

Don't you know the power of God? *He looks upon the earth, and makes it to tremble* (Ps 103.32). He commands, and the things that were shaken He makes firm once again. If He can make the quaking city to stand strong, much more can He make the Church stand strong![4]

The Church is stronger than Heaven: *Heaven and earth shall pass away, but My words shall never pass away* (Mt 24.35). What words? *You are Peter, and upon this Rock I will build My Church, and the gates of hell will not prevail against her* (Mt 16.18).

If you do not believe those words, believe the things He has done. How many tyrants have wanted to prevail over the Church? How many instruments of torture have been used? How many furnaces, wild beasts, sharpened swords? None of them has prevailed.

Where now are those who fought against her? Silenced, plunged into oblivion. And where is the Church? Shining more brightly than the sun. The attacks of her enemies have been vanquished, while her weapons are immortal. If when her numbers were few, they were not defeated, now that the whole world is filled with Christian devotion,

---

[4]He is referring to an actual earthquake that shook Constantinople some time previous. He soon refers again to the same event.

how is it possible to vanquish her? *Heaven and earth shall pass away, but My words will never pass away.*

And it's not hard to understand how the Church is more invincible than Heaven. For the Church is more greatly loved[5] by God than Heaven. For He did not take a body for the sake of Heaven; rather, He took flesh for the Church's sake. Heaven is for the Church; the Church is not for Heaven.

Don't be in an uproar over what I'm saying! Grace me with this—your unwavering faith. Don't you see Peter, venturing upon the water, then starting to doubt, and then starting to sink—not because of a change in the nature of the water, but because of the weakness of his faith?

Was it by the judgment of men that we have been brought to this point? Was it a man who led me here, to destroy me, a fellow human being? I say these things not out of madness—God forbid!—or out of pretension, but out of a desire to strengthen what has been shaken in you.

Since the city still stood after the earthquake, then the devil wanted to shake the Church. O polluted devil, more polluted than anything else, you did not prevail over the walls of the city, so do you now expect to shake the Church? Does the Church consist of walls? The Church consists of the multitude of believers. Behold what solid pillars there are in this temple—pillars not bound together by bands of iron, but tightly joined together by bonds of faith.

I'm not saying that this multitude is more powerful than fire, for they are still human; yet fire cannot destroy

[5]Greek: *potheinotera.*

them. Are you forgetting, O devil, how many wounds you inflicted upon the martyrs? How often a tender young virgin entered the arena, and though softer than wax she proved to be stronger than rock? How you tore her body but did not tear out her faith? How you wracked her body, but the power of her faith did not weaken? How you consumed her body, but did not disrupt her mindfulness? How you killed her body, but her piety remained?

You could not destroy one woman, and yet you expect to destroy this multitude? Have you not heard the Lord saying, *Where two or three are gathered together in My name, there I am in the midst of them* (Mt 18.20)? Do you imagine that when such a multitude is gathered, bound together by such love, that He is not here, too? I have His pledge; am I not able to put my full confidence in that?

I hold fast His Scriptures, which are my staff, my security, my calm harbor. Even if the whole world totters, I hold fast His Scriptures, which I know well, which are my wall and my stronghold. And what do they declare? *I am with you always, even unto the end of the age* (Mt 28.20).

Christ is with me; whom am I to fear? Even if waves rise up against me, even the whole ocean itself, and the wrath of rulers, this would all be as insignificant to me as a spider's web. And today, if it were not for your love, I would not hesitate to leave. Always I say, "Lord, Thy will be done."[6] Not what this one wants, or that one, but only what You want.

---

[6]Cf. Mt 6.10.

This is my fortress, this is my immovable rock, this is my unwavering staff. Whatever God wishes to happen, let it happen. If He wishes for me to remain here, I give thanks for that. If He wishes for me to be elsewhere, I give thanks for that as well.

Let no one trouble you; just devote yourselves to prayers. These things the devil has done, in order to cut short your zeal for prayer. But he will not succeed. Instead, we have found you to be more zealous, more fervent, in prayer.

Tomorrow I will go forth with you in liturgical prayer. Wherever I am, you will be there, too; wherever you are, I will be there also. We are one body; the body is not separated from the head, and neither is the head separated from the body. We may be separated in location, but our unity in love will never be broken. And neither will death be able to break us apart. For if my body dies, my soul still lives, and I will remember my people.

You are kinsmen unto me; how would I ever be able to forget you? You are kinsmen unto me; you are my life; you are my fulfillment. If you progress in spiritual things, I am well-pleased—since for me, the value of my life rests in your spiritual treasury. I am ready to be sacrificed for you ten thousand times—and in this I am not in any way bestowing a gift upon you. Rather, it's the debt I owe you: *For the good Shepherd lays down His life for the sheep* (Jn 10.11).

Dying as a sacrifice for you would be the basis for my immortality; their treachery against me would become the foundation of my eternal security. Is it because my possessions are plotted against that I lament? Is it because of my sins that I grieve? No, it's because of the love[7] that I have for you. For I do everything so that you will remain in security, so that no one will invade the sheepfold, so that the flock will remain unharmed. This motivation for enduring my struggles in itself suffices as my crown.

And why would I suffer for you? Because you are my fellow-citizens, you are my fathers, you are my brethren, you are my children, you are my members, you are my body, you are my light—a light sweeter even than the light of the sun. What can the rays of the sun mean to me compared to your love? For the sun's rays are only useful in this present life, while your love weaves for me a crown in the coming age!

I say these things in your hearing—and who could be more attentive than all of you? For so many days you have remained watchful, and nothing has slackened your vigilance. The passage of time has not made you softer; neither have fears or threats weakened you. You have become noble in the face of everything.

And why do I say, "You have *become*"? For what I have always desired you have accomplished—despising the things of this life, trampling upon the things of the earth, and transferring your attention to the things of Heaven. You have escaped the bonds of the body, striving to embrace that blessed heavenly philosophy.

---

[7]Greek: *erōta*.

These things are my crown, my comfort, my consolation, my anointing, my life, my foundation for immortality.[8]

[8]This sermon does not conclude in the customary way, since apparently at some later point another hand added the final two sections of this sermon as given in the *Patrologia Graeca*. Hence, a translation of these final two sections will not be included here—since by their variations in tone, content, grammar, and syntax, it is quite obvious that they do not convey authentic words of Chrysostom. His eminent biographer, J. N. D. Kelly, concurs: "In the closing two sections, the tone changes abruptly: John turns from affectionate pleading and exhortation to polemical abuse. These sections have come down to us in what seems to be two redactions which at points repeat, at points supplement each other. The text of both is confused, even chaotic; and the Greek seems occasionally hardly to make sense." Kelly, *Golden Mouth*, 230.

Oration upon His Return

A note on the text

Just a day after St John was sent off into exile, there was "a shaking" at night in the imperial bedroom, as reported by Chrysostom's biographer, Palladius.[1] This "shaking" was probably either Empress Eudoxia having a miscarriage, or her very young daughter having an accident that proved to be fatal. Whatever it was, the empress was immediately convinced that it must have been a sign of the Lord's displeasure for her role in exiling St John; and with tears and supplications, she convinced her husband Emperor Arcadius of the same thing.

So immediately, that very night, they had soldiers sent to bring John back to the capital, after giving them a letter from her for John, from which he quotes in the following

[1]Palladius, *Dialogus de vita Joannis Chrysostomi* 9 (the Greek is vague: *thrausin tina*); English translation: *Palladius: Dialogue on the Life of St. John Chrysostom*, trans. Robert T. Meyer, Ancient Christian Writers 45 (Mahwah, NJ: Paulist Press, 1985), 57.—*Ed.*

homily. After a delay of several days, and after receiving assurances that he would be fully and canonically reinstated by a church council to his position as archbishop of the city, he consented to come back.

His biographer, J. N. D. Kelly, describes what happened next:

> John's re-entry into the city in early October was a triumphal one. Writing to Pope Innocent of Rome, he simply recalls that the emperor had sent a secretary of the imperial consistory (*notarios*) to conduct him, and that more than thirty bishops came out to escort him. In fact, immense, exultant crowds received him, thronging the streets and squares, singing psalms and carrying lighted tapers....
>
> When the procession reached the Church of the Holy Apostles, the people, at John's bidding, swarmed into the church, where he delivered a short, extempore address; the Greek original is lost, but two independent Latin versions, which, it is generally agreed, reproduce its substance, survive. Recalling that he had used Job's exclamation, "Blessed be God," in his last sermon to them, he declares that he is glad to repeat the words now—"Blessed be God, who allowed me to go into exile; blessed also be God, who has ordered me to return." His enemies had hoped to separate him from his people, but their efforts had only won him more friends. Previously the

church alone had been filled; today the entire city square has been transformed into a church. Best of all, although there is horse-racing in the hippodrome, there are no spectators there; for everyone has thronged to church. What especially rejoices him is that, while the flock assembled here is so numerous, the wolves, the robbers, the adulterers who tried to seduce his bride [i.e., his flock] have all been dispersed. And they have been routed, not by any spear or sword of his, but by the tears and continuous prayers of his faithful people.[2]

The following Sunday, in spite of his initial refusal, with his reiterated protests that he must be officially rehabilitated before resuming his episcopal functions, he was prevailed upon, by popular demand, to take his seat on the throne of Hagia Sophia and, at the start of the service, to give the liturgical greeting "Peace be with you" to the congregation. This was a right reserved to the bishop,

---

[2]Here are some of the words he spoke at that moment: "The circumstances are different, but the praise to God (*doxologia*) is one and the same. I praised God when I was driven away, and I'm praising Him upon my return. The circumstances are different, but the purpose of both winter and summer is the same: the one purpose is the abundant fruit-bearing of the earth. Blessed be God who allowed my departure; blessed be God who called me back again! Blessed be God who permits the storm; blessed be God who dissipates it, making everything calm again! I'm saying these things to teach you to praise God [no matter what happens]." There is no Greek text of this speech given in the PG series; a Greek version, perhaps later translated from Latin, can be found in *Johannes Chrysostomi Opera Omnia*, vol. 3, ed. Montfaucon [Paris: Gaume Fratres, 1837], 506).

and his people's insistence that he should exercise it was a public acknowledgment that in their view his deposition was invalid.[3]

This is the homily he preached that Sunday, upon his return to his cathedral. He begins by comparing how an Egyptian Pharaoh almost ravished Abraham's wife (see Gen 12.10–20) with how another Egyptian, Archbishop Theophilus of Alexandria, almost ravished the Church of Constantinople by orchestrating the deposition of St John at the completely contrived and illegal Synod of the Oak.

[3]Kelly, *Golden Mouth*, 235–36.

Oration upon His Return[4]

When Pharaoh seized Sarah from Abraham; when the evil, barbaric Egyptian took this beautiful and graceful woman; when he beheld her beauty with unchaste eyes, wanting to commit an adulterous deed with her; God did not punish him right away. This was in order that the courage of the righteous man would be made manifest, as well as the prudence of the woman, and the licentiousness of the barbarian, and God's love for mankind—Abraham's courage, in that he bore what happened with thankfulness; Sarah's prudence, in that having fallen into the hands of the barbarian, she maintained her purity; Pharaoh's licentiousness, in that he threatened another's marriage-bed; and God's love for mankind, in that when the people were in despair, then He gave the crown [of victory] to the righteous one.

Back then, these things happened to Abraham; today, such things have happened to the Church. Then, it was Pharaoh; now, it's another Egyptian [Archbishop

[4]PG 52:443–48.

Theophilus of Alexandria]. Then, bodyguards; now, spearmen. Then, it was a woman who was [almost] ravished; now, it's the Church. Then, she was held for one night; now, he was gone away for one day.[5] And it was only for one day, so that the purity of the Bride [i.e., the Church] would be made manifest, in that while her pastor was gone, the beauty of her purity was not corrupted, despite the fact that he [Archbishop Theophilus] prepared the adultery and fulfilled the edicts, to which many in the imperial house subscribed.

The plot was devised, but its completion did not take place. That one's evil was revealed, as well as God's love for mankind. But that barbarian [Pharaoh], upon recognizing his sin, confessed his transgression; for he said to Abraham, *What have you done? Why did you not tell me she was your wife? I almost sinned* (Gen 12.18–19). But the one of our day [Archbishop Theophilus] remains in his sin. As God said to Cain, *O wretched, miserable one! You have sinned; be still* (Gen 4.7), so that he would not add sin upon sin.

Sarah arose, having Egyptian wealth; the Church rose up, having a wealth of knowledge, and manifestly more prudent. Behold the madness of the barbarian

[5]For dramatic effect, emphasizing the parallels between the two situations, St John uses the phrases "one night" and "one day." But he does so exaggeratedly, since the text in Genesis implies that Sarah was in Pharaoh's house for more than one night, and John was probably away from the city for at least a week—though it was the very next night after he was taken away into exile that the empress sent the soldiers to bring John back to the city.

[Archbishop Theophilus]. You cast out the shepherd; what flock did you tear apart? You removed the pilot; what tillers did you strike down? You cast out the vinedresser; what vines did you pull up?[6] What monasteries did you corrupt? I am speaking in the way of barbarians.

He did all this, so that your courage would be manifested.[7] He did all this, so that you might learn that this flock is shepherded by Christ. The shepherd was cast out, but the flock remained intact. Hence the apostolic words are fulfilled—*Not only in my presence, but also in my absence, work out your salvation with fear and trembling* (Phil 2.12).

They did such things, fearing your courage and the power of your love, your desire for me.[8] "We dare do nothing in the city," it says; "give Him to us outside it."[9] You received me outside the city,[10] so learn of the desire of the Church; learn of the nobility of my children, the strength

[6]St John is referring to himself here as the shepherd, pilot, and vinedresser of the Church of Constantinople, and he is exulting in the fact that his flock, including the monasteries, remained intact and unharmed even after his exile.

[7]Now St John is talking to his flock and referring to Theophilus.

[8]Greek: "power" (*philtron*), "love" (*pothon*).

[9]Perhaps St John is imagining what the Jewish leaders said to Judas before he betrayed Jesus to them near the Garden of Gethsemane outside the city of Jerusalem.

[10]Here St John is addressing Archbishop Theophilus and the others who had him deposed and exiled (though, of course, they were not present; Theophilus had already fled back to Alexandria). We recall that the infamous Synod of the Oak was held outside the city of Constantinople, in a suburb of Chalcedon on the eastern shore of the Bosphorus, across the water from Constantinople.

of the soldiers, the power of the armed men,[11] the brilliance of their crowns, the abundance of their wealth, the greatness of their love,[12] the steadfastness of their patience, the flower of freedom, the splendor of victory, the decisiveness of your defeat.

O new and paradoxical things! The shepherd is outside, and the flock dances; the general is far off, and the soldiers are well-armed. No longer did the Church only have her "encampment"; for the whole city became a church. The lanes, the marketplaces, the air were sanctified. The heretics repented; the Jews became better. The priests condemned,[13] while the Jews rejoiced in God, and ran to us.

So also it happened with Christ. Caiaphas crucified Him, and the thief confessed Him. O what a new and paradoxical thing! The priests killed, and the magi worshiped. But these things are not surprising in the Church. For if these things had not happened, our wealth would not have been revealed—it indeed would not have been revealed. For just as Job was righteous, but his righteousness would not have been made manifest without the wounds and the worms, so also our wealth would not have been made manifest without the plots; yes, it would not have been revealed. For God, in bringing Job to account, said, *Do you think that I judged you in any way other than justly?* (Job 40.8).

[11]Here St John refers to those in his flock who were armed with spiritual weapons.

[12]Greek: *agapēs.*

[13]Referring to the clergy who participated in his unjust deposition.

They plotted, they made war, they were defeated. How did they make war? With clubs. How were they defeated? By prayers. *If anyone strikes you on your right cheek, turn to him the other* (Mt 5.39). Yet you attack the Church with weapons, making war upon her.[14] Where peace should prevail, you start war, respecting neither the reverence of the place, O wretched and miserable one, nor the worthiness of the priesthood, nor the greatness of the authority here.

The baptistry was filled with blood.[15] In the place where sins are remitted, blood flowed. In what battle formation can such things happen? The emperor enters and puts aside his armor and his crown, while you entered wielding weapons. He left at the door the symbols of his power, while you came inside bearing the symbols of war. Did you think you would injure my Bride? She continues to show forth her beauty.

In this I rejoice, and not just that you, my flock, have conquered. For if I had been present, I would have had a part with you in the victory. But since I was away, your trophy is manifest as entirely yours. Yet this is the basis for my praise for you, in which I have a share with you in the victory; for you shone forth such nobility even in the absence of your father. Just as valiant athletes who demonstrate their prowess in the absence of their trainer,

[14]Again St John is addressing Theophilus *in absentia*.

[15]According to J. N. D. Kelly, St John is referring here to some monks loyal to Archbishop Theophilus who had entered the cathedral of Hagia Sophia and had physically attacked some of the parishioners loyal to St John, shedding their blood. Kelly, *Golden Mouth*, 233.

so you, in the absence of your teacher, have shown forth the nobility and comeliness of your own faith.

What more can I say? The very stones cry out, and the walls give voice. Go to the imperial palace, and you will hear: "O people of Constantinople! Go to the seaside, to the desert, to the mountains, to each house, and there your praise is recorded!"

How did you conquer? Not with engines of war, but with faith. O people who love their teacher! O people who love their father! Blessed is the city—not because of her columns and golden roofs, but because of your own virtue.

Such were the plots; but you conquered through prayer, and naturally so. For your prayers were lengthy, and fountains of your tears poured forth. They had spears, while you had tears; they had anger, while you had meekness. They tried to enforce their own will; you prayed for God's will to be done.

Where now are those who opposed you? Did we brandish weapons? Did we stretch out the bow? Did we hurl spears? No, we only prayed, and they fled. They were scattered like a spider's web, while you stood firm like a rock.

I am blessed through you. Before now, I knew I had a great amount of wealth because of you. But now, I marvel at you even more! We were far away, and the city was moved; for the sea became a city—all for one man! Women, men, very young children, women with their nurslings, daringly braved the sea, despising the waves.[16] Servants

---

[16]He is referring here to the people who went forth in boats to greet him and escort him upon his return from exile.

did not fear their master, and women forgot the weakness of their sex. The marketplace became a church—and all of this because of us.

To whom have we not given instruction through our example? You have received even the empress into your dance; I have not hidden her zeal. I do not say these things to punish her, but to foster her piety. For I have not hidden her zeal. She has not taken weapons in hand, but rather, righteous deeds of virtue.

Then I was sent into exile—you know how it happened. It is necessary to recount these sad events, in order for you to learn the benefits from them, and to learn more clearly how I was exiled, and how I returned.

They sowed with tears; they reaped in rejoicing. *They went forth and wept as they cast their seeds, but they shall return with rejoicing, bringing their sheaves* (Ps 125.5–6). These words have become reality for us. With thanksgiving you have received back the one you groaned for; you have accompanied him back to the city. And all this did not take a long time—in just one day it happened. The delay was for your sake, since God had it all arranged from the beginning.

I'm sharing with you paradoxical things. For though I was alone sailing on the sea, yet I was carrying the Church with me. For love[17] is not constricted, and neither was the ship too small. *For you are not constricted by us* (2 Cor 6.12a).

---

[17]Greek: *agapē*.

My solicitude for you endures; for though we were separated physically, we remained one in mind and heart. Having been sent away, I besought God to take care of you, my beloved flock; having been sent away, I kept thinking only of you, even while pondering upon our separation from one another.

Then suddenly, after only one day, our most God-loving empress sent a letter to me with these words that you should know of: "I was not aware of your sanctity, which events that have just happened have made known to me. I am innocent of your blood. For evil and corrupt men were the ones who engineered the plot. God is witness to my tears—this God whom I serve."

What libation did she pour out? Her tears were her libation. "This God whom I serve."[18] Hence, she is a priestess,[19] serving God with her own hands, and offering forth her tears and confession and repentance—not for herself, but for the Church, for the scattered people. She remembered, she remembered her own children and their Baptism; for she also wrote, "I remembered that my children were baptized by your own hands."[20]

Such was the conduct of our empress, while the priests who, out of envy, sent me into exile, did not even know the place where I was being sent. But wonderful to relate, she trembled for me as if for one of her own children and

[18]Greek: "serve" (*hiereuō*).

[19]The word *hiereuō* has the same root as the word for "priest" (*hiereus*), and means "to offer sacrifice."

[20]St John had personally baptized her children—the future St Pulcheria and the future Emperor Theodosius II.

looked everywhere for me—not doing so herself, but the soldiers whom she sent after me did so. She was trying to thwart the possibility that my enemies would even slay me, for they had spread out far and wide, seeking to destroy me.

Then on her knees she besought the emperor, clutching him, asking him to rescue me from their clutches—just as Abraham rescued Sarah from the clutches of the barbarian king. "We have lost our bishop!" she cried; "We must have him recalled! We will have no hope of retaining our royal authority if we do not have him returned! We must have nothing more to do with those who perpetrated this crime against him."

And her tears kept falling as she kept beseeching God that her goal would be attained. You yourselves know how much benevolence we have received from her, how she has taken us into her own embrace, and how she has spoken up for you, hastening to assist you.

And she did not forget your good-will towards her, for you extolled her as the mother of the churches, a provider for the monasteries, a protector of the saints, a staff of the poor. Her praise is the glory of God, the crown of the churches.

Have I mentioned her fervent love?[21] Have I spoken of her kind liberality[22] towards me? Yesterday, in the depths of the night, she sent messengers to me with these words: "Tell him that my prayer is full, I have done the right thing,

[21]Greek: *pothon.*
[22]Greek: *philotimian.*

I have a better crown than the royal diadem—for I have called back our bishop. I have been given back the head of the Body, the pilot of the ship, the shepherd of the flock, the bridegroom of the nuptial chamber."

The adulterers are covered with shame. And whether I live, or whether I die, it no longer means anything to me. Behold the value of trials!

What will I do, in order to repay you with a reward worthy of your love[23] for me? I am not able to give anything worthy; but what I have, I give. For I love to readily pour out my blood for your salvation.

No one else has such children, no one else has such a flock, no one else has a field so abundantly thriving! And there is no need for me to cultivate the land, for I can sleep, and the grain will flourish.[24] There is no need for me to labor, for I can be silent, and the sheep will escape from the wolves.

What will I call you? Sheep or shepherds, sailors or pilots, soldiers or generals? You prove all of these words to be true. For when I see your good order, I call you sheep. When I see your foresight, I address you as shepherds. When I see your wisdom, I name you pilots. When I see your courage and athletic prowess, I say that you all are soldiers and generals.

O the labor, O the foresight of the people! You have chased away the wolves, yet you are still being vigilant.

[23]Greek: *agapēs*.
[24]A possible allusion to Mark 4.26–29.

Those who "sailed" with you turned against you; they prepared for war in the "ship" of the Church. Cry out for those clergy to be expelled, and for other ones to take their place in the Church.

But is there a need to cry out? They have gone away; they have been driven out; they have taken flight, without anyone following them. And all this, with no one accusing them—only their own conscience. *If an enemy had reproached me, I would have borne it* (Ps 54.12).

Those who were with us turned against us. Those who piloted the ship with us wanted to capsize it.[25] I have marveled at your wisdom in resisting their machinations. And I say these things, not to stir you to revolt. For rebellion was their part, while zeal for truth was yours. You never esteemed those who were rising up; rather, you hindered them, both on behalf of your own well-being and that of the Church, lest the "ship" be submerged once again.

Your courage did not permit the storm to rage, while their plan was to bring the waves over the ship. And I ponder not upon what could have happened, but upon their plan that was thwarted.

O man standing by the altar, bearing the accusation of such a people! When you should have been putting the evils in check, you fomented the storm, you turned the sword against yourself, you destroyed your own children, in thought if not in deed.[26] But God prevented that.

---

[25]Here he is most probably referring to those fellow clergy, bishops and priests, who had turned against him at the Synod of the Oak.

[26]Again, St John is addressing Theophilus.

So I marvel at you all, and praise you, that after the war you are making sure there is strong and lasting peace. For it is necessary that the pilot and the sailors be of one mind;[27] for if they are in dissension, the vessel will capsize.

So consolidate the peace, with the grace of God. And I will make you all sharers in my security. Yet I will be able to do nothing without you, along with the most God-loving empress. For she takes thought and care, and does everything to make the vineyard secure, to assure that the Church remains unshaken by storms.

So I extol your wisdom, and I also praise the foresight of our imperial rulers. For they have shown more concern about dissensions in the Church than about any war, and more solicitude for the well-being of the Church than for that of the capital city.[28]

---

[27] Greek: *homonoian*.

[28] St John is trying very hard to show his good-will and his complete lack of resentment to the imperial couple, especially Empress Eudoxia, knowing full well that she and her husband Emperor Arcadius both had a major role in his exile. But surely he was hoping that his forgiveness and his praise for their former support of him and the Church would encourage them to be supportive of his ministry in the capital city going forward. Very sadly, however, in June of the next year (404), Empress Eudoxia did not try to prevent his second exile when her husband finally issued that order, having weakened under extreme pressure from a number of local bishops hostile to Chrysostom. St Palladius, St John's close friend and biographer, predicted that those who contributed to John's second and final exile would die shortly thereafter. As things happened, Empress Eudoxia died only four months after John was sent into his final exile, and Emperor Arcadius died less than four years later, at the age of 31.

So let us invoke God, let us highly esteem the Church, let us remain steadfast in prayer—lest, having been delivered from disasters, we become foolishly complacent.

Up to this day, we have prayed for deliverance from disasters. So now let us give thanks to God; and let us now be as zealous for the good as we have been courageous before now.

For all of this, let us give thanks to God, to whom be glory and might, together with the Son, and the good and life-giving Spirit, now and ever, and unto ages of ages. Amen.

POPULAR PATRISTICS SERIES

ST VLADIMIR'S SEMINARY PRESS
1-800-204-2665 • www.svspress.com

We hope this book has been enjoyable and edifying for your spiritual journey toward our Lord and Savior Jesus Christ.

One hundred percent of the net proceeds of all SVS Press sales directly support the mission of St Vladimir's Orthodox Theological Seminary to train priests, lay leaders, and scholars to be active apologists of the Orthodox Christian Faith. However, the proceeds only partially cover the operational costs of St Vladimir's Seminary. To meet our annual budget, we rely on the generosity of donors who are passionate about providing theological education and spiritual formation to the next generation of ordained and lay servant leaders in the Orthodox Church.

Donations are tax-deductible and can be made at www.svots.edu/donate. We greatly appreciate your generosity.

To engage more with St Vladimir's Orthodox Theological Seminary, please visit:

www.svots.edu
online.svots.edu
www.svspress.com
www.instituteofsacredarts.com